"This book highlights the clash between the church and our culture and how we should respond to these challenges. The author explains that we are called to rescue the culture, not just preach to it. He illustrates this by detailing many of the cultural trends we face and their impact on the church and how we must address them. This is a reminder that the church is the hope of the world and, as such, we are called to influence culture rather than submit to its pressures."

—DR. ERWIN LUTZER, senior pastor, Moody Church, Chicago

"Michael Craven has invested years in research, writing, and travel to address cultural issues in our day while identifying the most strategic battleground: the mind. A dynamic apologist, Michael separates the external cultural context from essential Christian truth and brings the reader the single, specific, and stirring challenge to think biblically."

—DR. DAVID H. MCKINLEY, pastor, Warren Baptist Church, Augusta, Georgia

"Michael Craven is a fresh voice who avoids the common dangers in dealing with hot-button ideas in both the culture and the church. This book is representative of a new kind of apologetics that is desperately needed. Careful readers will be rewarded by investing serious thought in this fine book."

—JOHN H. ARMSTRONG, president, ACT 3

"A book by an American about America and for Americans in the light of God's Word. Michael's incisive critique, biblical wisdom, and deep compassion have produced a work that needs to be read and processed by many. I heartily agree with and support his message."

—STUART MCALLISTER, vice president of training and special projects, RZIM

"Believing Scripture to be truth without any mixture of error, S. Michael Craven applies Truth to the error of our age. He helps the reader wade through the brackish mixture of current thought to distinguish the pure water of the Word."

—DR. JACK GRAHAM, pastor, Prestonwood Baptist Church, Plano, Texas

UNCOMPROMISEDFAITH

OVERCOMING OUR CULTURALIZED CHRISTIANITY

S. MICHAEL CRAVEN

NAVPRESS

NAVPRESS ◐®

NavPress is the publishing ministry of The Navigators, an international Christian organization and leader in personal spiritual development. NavPress is committed to helping people grow spiritually and enjoy lives of meaning and hope through personal and group resources that are biblically rooted, culturally relevant, and highly practical.

**For a free catalog go to www.NavPress.com
or call 1.800.366.7788 in the United States or 1.800.839.4769 in Canada.**

© 2009 by S. Michael Craven

All rights reserved. No part of this publication may be reproduced in any form without written permission from NavPress, P.O. Box 35001, Colorado Springs, CO 80935. www.navpress.com

NAVPRESS and the NAVPRESS logo are registered trademarks of NavPress. Absence of ® in connection with marks of NavPress or other parties does not indicate an absence of registration of those marks.

ISBN-13: 978-1-60006-362-6

Cover design by The DesignWorks Group, Tim Green
Cover image by Getty Images, Dwight Eschliman

Some of the anecdotal illustrations in this book are true to life and are included with the permission of the persons involved. All other illustrations are composites of real situations, and any resemblance to people living or dead is coincidental.

Unless otherwise identified, all Scripture quotations in this publication are taken from: the *Holy Bible: New International Version*® (NIV®). Copyright © 1973, 1978, 1984 by International Bible Society. Used by permission of Zondervan. All rights reserved. Other versions used include the Holy Bible, English Standard Version (ESV), copyright © 2001 by Crossway Bibles, a division of Good News Publishers. Used by permission. All rights reserved; the New King James Version (NKJV). Copyright © 1982 by Thomas Nelson, Inc. Used by permission. All rights reserved; and the King James Version.

Library of Congress Cataloging-in-Publication Data

Craven, S. Michael, 1960-
  Uncompromised faith : overcoming our culturalized Christianity / S. Michael Craven.
    p. cm.
  ISBN-13: 978-1-60006-362-6
  ISBN-10: 1-60006-362-4
  1. Christianity and culture--United States. I. Title.
  BR517.C73 2009
  261.0973--dc22

                         2008027640

Printed in the United States of America

1 2 3 4 5 6 7 8 / 13 12 11 10 09

To my precious wife and partner, Carol, and my children, Tyler, Catherine, and Maddie: You are all a part of God's abundant grace and generous blessing to me. Thank you for your support, your patience, and, above all, your indulgence of my inattention while writing this book.

CONTENTS

FOREWORD

For years there has been an increasing concern with the state of the church in America and its growing irrelevance both here and throughout the Western world.

Research reveals that Christianity in America has become more diluted, more distorted, and less Christlike with each subsequent generation. Heterodoxy is replacing orthodoxy, and the notion of absolute truth has been all but eliminated from popular thinking. And our young people, raised in Christian homes, are walking away from the church in alarming numbers. So severe is the crisis that I dared to proclaim that if something serious does not occur in the life of the church, we may be witnessing the last Christian generation in America.

Increasingly, Americans no longer hold to what evangelicals consider to be the true foundations of the Christian faith. The theological ignorance and biblical illiteracy of this generation are possibly the worst in history—an astonishing fact when you consider that we are the most educationally resource-rich generation in the history of the church. The net effect is a generation that professes Christ but doesn't follow Him. Christianity, for many, has become a private matter, based more on simple assent to a few facts about Jesus: Pray "the Sinner's Prayer," and you're done! But this is a far cry from the historic Christian faith that has been transforming people and the world for nearly two thousand years.

For centuries, Christians have been formulating and presenting a serious interpretation of reality that was applied to every aspect of life and culture. This interpretation, or Christian worldview, once shaped the cultural institutions of the Western world as well as the social and moral consensus. However, a serious shift began in the latter part of the eighteenth century, the effects of which continue to this day. Following the Enlightenment, Christianity began to be supplanted by new ideas about life and reality—ideas that sought to elevate man and eliminate God. Initially, this challenge was met by serious and intellectually formidable Christians. However, by the end of the nineteenth century, an anti-intellectual spirit began to dominate the American church, and Christians had less and less to offer in the way of serious ideas about life and the world. The result: The church and Christianity ceased to influence the culture and instead became increasingly conformed to the culture.

In the pages that follow, Michael meticulously peels back the layers of today's culture to expose the manner and means of Christianity's unwitting cultural captivity in America, offering a thoughtful route to reform rooted in historic orthodoxy. This book will challenge you to think deeply about the times and culture in which you live and how these conditions have combined to shape our thinking in ways that inhibit an authentic and robust Christian life.

Every Christian needs to read this book if he or she wants to understand the times in which we live and how to live faithfully within them.

—JOSH MCDOWELL, speaker and author

ACKNOWLEDGMENTS

Some of the ideas in the first chapter were sharpened and aided by the writings of, conversations with, and influence of my brother-in-law, Peter Hansen. I am grateful for his intellect, scholarship, insight, and contribution. I am also grateful for the influence of Mardi Keyes at L'Abri Fellowship in Massachusetts, whose insight into Christian feminism was profoundly helpful and challenged many of my own cultural assumptions. I am indebted to my editors—Jamie, for her relentless charge to make this the best book possible, and Caleb, who raised the bar and held it there! Last, I am grateful to the board of directors for the Center for Christ and Culture for their enthusiastic support and encouragement, without whom this book would not have been realized. To John, Kevin, Chris, Scott, and Dianne: Thank you!

INTRODUCTION

I recall seeing the sci-fi action film *The Matrix*, starring Keanu Reeves, when it was first released in 1999. For those of you unfamiliar with the film, it portrays a future in which reality, as perceived by humans, is actually the product of an artificially constructed computer program called the Matrix. This false reality, in which people think they are living ordinary lives, is created by sentient machines to pacify and subdue the human population while their bodies' heat and electrical activity are used as an energy source. As the story unfolds, Thomas Anderson (Keanu Reeves), a computer hacker who operates under the name Neo, begins receiving cryptic messages on his computer, encouraging him to ask, "What is the Matrix?" Soon Neo encounters several sinister "agents" concerned about his interest in the Matrix. He is rescued by a small band of rebel humans led by the mysterious Morpheus (Laurence Fishburne).

Neo is brought to Morpheus, who asks him, "Do you want to know the truth?" Morpheus's hanging question is followed by a choice: take the blue pill and all will return to normal with no recollection of the experience, and life will simply go on as it has always been; or take the red pill and the truth will be revealed. Before Neo chooses, Morpheus warns that if the red pill is chosen, there can be no going back, its effect irreversible. If the red pill is chosen, Neo will discover the truth and bear the full weight of its consequences. Of course, Neo chooses the red pill and discovers the horrible reality of humanity's condition—that they are in bondage to this malevolent society of machines.

What follows is nothing short of a radical adjustment in Neo's worldview. Everything he has previously understood and believed to be the truth about reality is, in fact, a lie; his life from this point forward will never be the same. Something extraordinary that can never be undone has taken place in Neo's life, so much so that the whole of his existence from that point forward will be dedicated to liberating others in light of this truth.

I could not help but draw parallels between this story and that of conversion to faith in Jesus Christ. All that we have previously understood about life and reality is shattered by the inbreaking reality of Christ. Upon receiving Christ as Lord and Savior, one cannot simply go on as if something extraordinary has not happened. This divine penetration into one's present reality—through which our eyes are opened, our own rebellion quelled, and we see or at least acknowledge for the first time that Jesus Christ has saved us from a horrible condition and dreadful fate—is the most amazing experience in any human life.

Everything we know changes! (Or it should.) All of our conceptions of reality, self, human nature, knowledge, morality, and ethics are thrown into a new understanding. We are, for the first time, truly alive in Christ, now able to obtain a new understanding of everything, the knowledge of which transforms us and how we live. The result of this radical transformation then bears witness to the life-changing truth, power, and presence of Jesus Christ. This transformation affects not only us personally but also our ideas about everything else—in other words, a new and true interpretation of reality. Sadly, it seems that in America this transformation has become something less in its witness-bearing power. This has not always been the case in our culture. Historically, Christians have been formidable in projecting this new and true interpretation of reality into every aspect of American life and culture — not by political coercion but through intellectual influence, missional activity, and compassionate outreach.

However, something has changed, producing a domesticated and irrelevant form of American Christianity that knows little, acts sporadically, and loves less — a culturalized Christianity that bears little resemblance to the historic orthodox faith. Our cultural institutions, which were once generally Christian in their ideas and practices, are now radically secular. The moral consensus has degenerated from universal virtues to individualized values, in which any and every moral persuasion is encouraged and tolerated. Any attempt to assert Christian ideas in the public square is either ignored or opposed. In short, Christianity has become irrelevant in shaping American life in any meaningful way.

In many ways, the times in which we live are not dissimilar to those of the sixteenth-century Reformers. Like us, they found themselves living in a cultural context in which Christianity had been systematically reduced to little more than religious ritual and personal piety. With societal emphasis on religious practice and outward behavior, they'd lost the majesty and radical reality of God's amazing grace — grace that not only transforms our outward behavior but also reorients every aspect of our lives and thinking. Similarly, we find ourselves living within a cultural context in which the majesty and radical reality of God's amazing grace has been subdued, culturalized, and rendered largely impotent — in other words, "having the appearance of godliness, but denying its power" (2 Timothy 3:5, ESV). It is the contributing causes of this condition that I seek to explore in hopes of identifying and tearing down what I have come to believe are deeply entrenched and rarely examined cultural barriers to both the acceptance of the gospel and the mission of the church in America.

PART I

Cultural Ideas That Hinder Belief
and Adversely Influence the
Christian Life and Witness

CHAPTER 1

The Crisis Confronting the American Church:
Rethinking Cultural Engagement

Looking back over the last two millennia of Western history, one cannot help but be impressed with the role Christianity has played in shaping and forming, for better or worse, this great civilization. Throughout the centuries, Christianity has faced enormous struggles. From virtual obscurity, Christianity rose to challenge and conquer one of the greatest empires the world has ever seen: the Roman Empire. Christianity served to civilize and educate an entire continent; it gave birth to the modern ideals of freedom, human dignity, equality, free market economics, and social justice. Christianity forever established as universal human virtues the concepts of compassion, love, sacrifice, and forgiveness. The monuments of Christianity can still be seen everywhere: from the cathedrals of Europe to the music of Bach; from the intellectual heritage of Augustine, Aquinas, and Calvin to the literature of Dante, Milton, and Shakespeare. From the colonization of America to the abolition of slavery, Christianity has been the most powerful and, one might add, most positive, formative influence on culture in the history of the world.

It has been the unique influence of Christianity that has produced the greatness of so-called Western civilization. However, I must stress that we are not to confuse Christianity and Western civilization, or being Christian with being American, as these are by no means synonymous. Christianity stands on its own, and where Christianity flourishes it naturally brings with it personal, social, and cultural transformation. Conversely, where Christianity fails to flourish or, more specifically, where the followers of Christ fail to think and act faithfully, cultures will likewise decline or fall short of their potential. This point was recently reinforced when a leading scholar from the Chinese Academy of Social Sciences, speaking to a group of Westerners in 2002, said,

> *One of the things we were asked to look into was what accounted for the success, in fact, the pre-eminence of the West all over the world. We studied everything we could from the historical, political, economic, and cultural perspective. At first, we thought it was because you had more powerful guns than we had. Then we thought it was because you had the best political system. Next we focused on your economic system. But in the past twenty years, we have realized that the heart of your culture is your religion: Christianity. That is why the West has been so powerful. The Christian moral foundation of social and cultural life was what made possible the emergence of capitalism and then the successful transition to democratic politics. We don't have any doubt about this.*[1]

This Chinese scholar acknowledges the obvious historical facts only when he recognizes that Christianity has been the central forming influence of the world's most successful civilization. Frankly, this success is an inevitable result for any civilization that, first, builds and maintains its social and cultural foundations upon truth that is consistent with reality and, second, rightfully acknowledges the source of this truth.

CHRISTIANITY IN TWENTY-FIRST-CENTURY AMERICA

So here at the dawn of the twenty-first century, what has become of Christianity in the West? What new struggles does it face? What can be said for Christianity in Western civilization and specifically in America as we look to the future?

In comparison with its past achievements, it is safe to say that evangelical Christianity today is in a pathetic state of decadence and decline in the West. It is, to a large degree, fragmented, watered-down, and retreating from relevancy. For the past two centuries, too many evangelical Christians have lived on the periphery of responsible intellectual and cultural existence. We have traded in Milton's *Paradise Lost* for *Left Behind*, the arias of Bach for contemporary Christian music, and Rembrandt for Thomas Kinkade. It is not my intention to denigrate Tim LaHaye or Jerry Jenkins, the contemporary Christian music industry, or Mr. Kinkade. However, the fact of the matter is that much of what passes for Christian art and literature today fails to rise to the same level of quality and achievement as that of historical Christian artists and writers. It is this substandard quality that necessitates the subcultural category now necessary to identify Christian art and literature as its own category.

So-called Christian art and literature no longer serves as the creative benchmark for mainstream art and culture. The fields of creative and intellectual expression once dominated by Christians have been largely abandoned, taking with them any objective standards by which we can judge the true, the good, and the beautiful. Modern evangelical Christianity has to a large extent become pietistic and legalistic; it has forgotten beauty, relativized truth, and, in many respects, reduced Jesus into nothing more than a marketing tool to sell music, T-shirts, and jewelry to an increasingly irrelevant subculture. Even the most casual observer of society and culture surely must recognize that consciously Christian ideas and values no longer direct any of our cultural institutions. The trend of every institution of American culture over the last fifty years has been a decidedly liberal drift, including some mainline Christian denominations. Welcome to post-Christian America!

Instead of engaging the intellectual and cultural challenges that we must in order to be salt and light in a world desperate for hope and meaning, the vast majority of evangelical Christians have abandoned the hard work of apprehending and pressing the truth into every sphere of life and culture. As a result, we have surrendered, by default, our influence in society to secular humanists and others who reject the truth and centrality of Christ to all of life.

From the public school system to the universities, the sciences to the humanities, films to the fine arts, politics to philosophy, Christians have, for the most part, abandoned mainstream culture and withdrawn to the confines of their churches, creating an elaborate Christian subculture with its own language, symbols, entertainment, and literature. To think, then, that we can venture out into the "real" world from this irrelevant subculture and reach people with the truth of Christ is naïve. The fact that the most important truth ever revealed to humanity has been successfully consigned to the margins of society has only strengthened the implausibility of the gospel story!

In the meantime, the truth claims of Christianity have come under vicious attack from all sides. The possibility of miracles, divine revelation, and the Incarnation is both questioned and categorized as a primitive, out-of-date interpretation of reality. The deity of Christ and the existence of God are either rejected altogether or reduced to a practical deism in which God set things in motion but has little to do with everyday life and social existence. The historical and scientific accuracy of the Bible is repeatedly attacked. One only has to recall the recent wave of critics and so-called theologians who weighed in on Mel Gibson's *The Passion of the Christ* or recent prime-time specials on Jesus and Paul—all dismissing the historical and supernatural truth of the biblical revelation and Jesus as God. The success of *The Da Vinci Code*, by Dan Brown, with its outrageous and false claims of conspiracy and cover-up as the impetus for the early founding of Christianity, promises to further weaken the plausibility of the Christian faith and message.

The way of salvation — through Christ alone — is regarded as divisive, offensive, or simply unnecessary. Competing religious systems are set over and against Christianity as being more tolerant and more humane. Today, Christians are often labeled fundamentalist right-wing extremists. Unfortunately, due to the general intellectual weakness and pervasive theological ignorance of the church, this is a label that is all too often accurate. And more and more, all remnants of our nation's Christian heritage are being systematically removed from the public square.

AN ANTI-INTELLECTUAL SPIRIT

Rather than engage these kinds of arguments and actions intelligently as 1 Peter 3:15 commands, many evangelicals continue to hide away under the mask of anti-intellectualism. Too many Christians think, *Apologetics is too rationalistic, cerebral, intellectual, and abstract. I don't need to try to rationally prove the existence of God or argue with others about whether or not He exists. I just need to show love and compassion. After all, what really matters is faith, hope, and love — not reason.* Reason, they say, just gets in the way of faith, hope, and love. They follow God with their heart, not their head! Others will retreat into the abyss of fideism, saying, *Religion is a matter of faith and cannot be argued by reason — one must simply believe.* Faith, they think, is a blind leap in the dark, devoid of any rational reasons. They argue that faith and reason stand opposed to one another. This might account for the lack of biblical literacy evident among so many professing Christians today. Recently George Barna reported that "75 percent of Americans believe that the Bible teaches that 'God helps those who help themselves'"![12]

This same attitude is to blame for the overwhelming absence of a consciously Christian life and worldview within the church, without which the Christian lacks the necessary theological framework for analyzing, understanding, and addressing every aspect of life, society, and culture from a coherent biblical philosophy. I will address this in greater detail later.

Nonetheless, this anti-intellectual attitude simply flies in the face of what the Bible teaches. We are commanded to "always be ready to give a defense to everyone who asks you a reason for the hope that is in you" (1 Peter 3:15, NKJV) or to "demolish arguments and every pretension that sets itself up against the knowledge of God . . . [taking] captive every thought to make it obedient to Christ" (2 Corinthians 10:5). This passage in 2 Corinthians is critical and is one we often either misunderstand or misapply. The apostle Paul is urging Christians to engage in intellectual discourse and persuasive debate whenever they find themselves confronted by false ideas that contradict the biblical understanding of life and reality. This passage is not to be understood in purely individualistic or private terms related to taking our *own* thoughts captive; we need to understand the ideas and thoughts of others that keep *them* from the knowledge of the truth. Practically speaking, this means we are to be actively engaged in pressing God's truth into every aspect of life and the world. N. T. Wright was helpful in further explaining the Christian's proper relationship to the world in which he or she lives:

> *The new life of the Spirit, to which Christians are called in the present age, is not a matter of sitting back and enjoying the spiritual comforts in a private, relaxed, easygoing spirituality, but consists rather of the unending struggle in the mystery of prayer,* the struggle to bring God's wise, healing order into the world now, *in implementation of the victory of the cross and anticipation of the final redemption.*[3] *(emphasis added)*

Rather than living and thinking consistent with the way God intends the world to be, modern Christians seem to be more comfortable with the way the world presently is. Thus, they remain uninterested in engaging in the hard task of reasoning, thinking, and earnestly contending for the faith that has been delivered once and for all to the saints!

OVERCOMING EMPTY-HEADED EVANGELICALISM

So what is to be done? Is there a way out of this destructive malaise of "empty-headed" evangelicalism? I believe the proper remedy is the repudiation of all types of anti-intellectualism that dumb down Christian theology, impoverish the witness of Christianity, and give Christians excuses not to ask and answer the hard questions.

The study of historic Christian apologetics is essential for any person who professes to be a follower of Christ. However, I want to make a distinction between historic Christian apologetics and cultural apologetics. Without venturing into the debate over classical, presuppositional, and evidential apologetics, let me just say that I believe that elements of each are helpful and not necessarily mutually exclusive. So when I use the term *historic Christian apologetics*, I am referring to those three schools of thought collectively. For the sake of understanding, classical apologetics "stresses rational arguments for the existence of God and historical evidences supporting the truth of Christianity."[4] Presuppositional apologetics differs in that it "defends Christianity from the departure point of certain basic presuppositions"[5]—namely, that all persons presuppose or assume certain explanations about reality that arise from their worldview. In presuppositionalism, the Christian apologist presents the truth of Christianity by exposing the fallacy of alternative worldviews, which the skeptic ultimately knows serve only to suppress the truth that in his heart he knows to be true. Finally, evidential apologetics stresses the need to first logically establish the existence of God before arguing for the truth of Christianity. Suffice it to say, these, to one degree or another, are all vital for the Christian to apprehend and be able to communicate.

But I want to emphasize the need for what can be called a "cultural" or "missional" apologetic. These work on two intellectual fronts. The first front addresses the ideas or ideological influences common to a given culture. These ideas surreptitiously shape our thinking in an osmotic fashion, like the water in which a fish swims: The fish doesn't give the water the slightest thought; it simply takes the water for granted. Such is the case with the ideas common to our culture. They are the air we breathe, and thus we scarcely give them a thought, but their influence on our thoughts, if unchecked, is formidable.

The second front pertains to social issues and their underlying ideas or worldview. These are most often expressed in the cultural debates over moral and ethical questions such as abortion, same-sex marriage, feminism, and homosexuality, to name just a few. The respective positions often represent opposing views of reality and the nature of man, yet whichever moral perspective—and its underlying worldview—gains social acceptance tends to form the consensus view of reality.

SENT INTO THE WORLD ON A MISSION

It is not enough to simply understand these two ideological fronts; a cultural apologetic ultimately relies on a missional approach to culture in order to effectively confront and subvert these ideas. Currently, we toss "Christian hand grenades," occasionally entering the culture to present our one-sided arguments for the truth of Christianity and then retreating to our churches as soon as we are done. Being missional means we act more like a rescue force that is determined to stay until all are rescued than like a commando unit that occasionally enters hostile territory to harass the enemy! Being missional means we endeavor to develop real and meaningful relationships with those who God, in His providence, has brought into our lives—to first demonstrate the love of Christ and then be ready with an answer to explain the hope that is within us. It means we listen more than we speak; we ask and answer questions and expand our conversations to include more than just religion; and when we speak—for goodness' sake!—we speak in normal language and not "Christianese."

The missional Christian presses into the world wherever he or she is and pushes back the darkness with the love of Christ. The missional Christian works at really getting to know and love his neighbor, not because he has to but because he loves people as Christ commanded. This includes those neighbors who are different, difficult, or just downright unlikeable. And, yes, this includes those neighbors who share very different political views and lifestyles. In other words, we really seek to interact and develop real relationships with the lost. It means we invite sinners into our life. It means we put up with their profanity and coarse talk. It means we love them as Christ loves them, without reservation. This is what it means to be missional. If you claim to be Christian, it is what you already are: a follower of Christ left on mission in hostile territory.

If you are armed with an understanding of the cultural and social barriers that inhibit the reception of the gospel and employ this missional approach, you will go a long way toward demonstrating the relevance of Christ and His message to the unbelieving world. It is the true mark of the Christian: love. It will also align your life with Christ's commandments.

A MISSIONAL EXAMPLE

I want to share an experience I had several years ago when speaking at the University of California–Berkeley that illustrates this missional approach. I had been invited by the student chapter of the ACLU to participate in a debate on same-sex marriage. Lucky me!

Now, let me be honest: UC–Berkeley was the last place on earth I wanted to go to defend the biblical perspective on marriage. However, God is providential, and I believed this was precisely where He wanted me to go, so I agreed. I would be joined in the debate by another Christian from a large pro-family organization, and we would be facing two gay activists from two organizations working to advance same-sex marriage. As I was flying from Dallas to Berkeley, I was praying for courage and wisdom. I confess there was an element of fear and I was not particularly enthusiastic about what awaited me later that evening.

As I was praying, the safety information card in the seat-back pocket in front of me caught my eye. Specifically, it was what I saw at the top of the card: REV. 11/3, referring to the date of its last revision. However, my first thought was that the Lord was directing me to Revelation 11:3. Of course, my rational side pushed this thought aside, but the Lord persisted, and I felt I must read this passage. I opened my Bible to find these words: "I will give power to my two witnesses." Wow! Needless to say, I was now a little more enthusiastic. As I continued to pray, the Lord brought to mind the differences in our respective goals for this event, His and mine. I wanted to win! I wanted to systematically, methodically, and intellectually destroy the opposition, demonstrating the superiority of the biblical perspective and, frankly, my own, as well. However, the Lord helped me see that this was not *His* purpose. I was reminded of God incarnate, Christ who humbled Himself unto death. This, I felt, was what the Lord was asking me to do — to surrender *my* ambitions and *my* goals of winning and instead present myself as a living sacrifice for His glory. In essence, the Lord was asking me if I was willing to be obedient to the point of public humiliation in order to demonstrate His love for His name's sake. This changed my whole approach from that of polemic argumentation to seeking humbly to persuade in an attitude of love, not opposition.

There were more than eight hundred students and faculty on hand. There was not an empty seat in the auditorium; every inch of floor space was occupied, as well as the perimeter walls. The place was packed! I can safely say that of the hundreds in the audience, only four were there in support of our position. How do I know this? I invited two and my partner invited the other two. This was the most hostile audience I had ever encountered in my life, and the debate hadn't even officially begun!

The debate began and I led off. I tried to limit my statements to the positive affirmations of traditional marriage and the natural family as supported by historical, sociological, and anthropological evidence. (These same arguments have been incorporated here into the subsequent chapter on marriage.) I most definitely did not employ any religious language. Once the crowd saw that I wasn't going to beat them over the head with Scripture and biblical moral arguments, they began to settle down, although I am speaking relatively. Then it was the opposition's turn, and their approach was not surprising. By slinging *ad hominem* insults and sarcasm, they incited the audience into a frenzy. Suffice it to say, this was not what I wanted to be a part of.

Then it was my partner's turn. To my dismay, he led off by quoting Romans chapter 1, and the reaction was unlike anything I had ever seen. The audience was screaming, laughing, booing, hissing—it was almost demonic. The debate continued for another hour, but honestly I was ready to leave after the first outburst. This had turned into a spectacle intended for the amusement of the audience, who in this case wanted to be entertained by the public humiliation of these Christians. I was thinking, *Lord, where are they seeing Your love in this?* I was grieved by the whole experience and wanted it to end.

Of course, it did end. As I was gathering up my things and preparing to leave the stage, I noticed a large crowd of students pressing toward me. Somewhat unsure of their motives at this point, I was greeted by the first student, a female. This young woman had virtually everything on her face pierced, and her T-shirt clearly proclaimed her sexual orientation, which was *not* heterosexual. However, much to my surprise, she thrust out her hand and said, "Mr. Craven, I want to thank you for coming. I didn't agree with everything you said, but you made some good points, and I really appreciated *the way* you spoke, unlike this @#*&! here," referring rather uncharitably to my partner. Not surprisingly, he quickly left the auditorium. This same pattern was repeated as student after student came forward to express thanks. Then a young woman came forward saying she was a Christian who had been living in a same-sex relationship for more than three years. She said, "I don't understand how something that feels so right to me could be wrong in the sight of God," and she began to weep. My heart broke for this young woman who was so obviously conflicted. Without going into great detail, I began to gently explain the biblical admonitions against her lifestyle while sympathizing with the reality of her attractions; I likened these to the sexual attraction felt by heterosexuals outside the context of a biblically prescribed relationship. I explained that acting upon these attractions outside the biblical prescription is an act of disobedience against God. At this point, I realized that I had reached across the podium and taken this young woman's hand as she wept. This moment was, for me, frozen as I looked up to observe the entire group of fifty to sixty students captivated by this exchange. It was as if the Lord said to me, *This is what I want them to see—that I love them and I died for them.*

I spent the next hour and a half with this entire group of young people, none of whom was Christian as far as I could tell, in the most productive and respectful dialogue I have ever experienced. These students had serious questions that I sensed they had been holding in reserve for years. It was as if they wanted to ask questions about Christianity but had never met a Christian, or a least one they were inclined to speak with. As the evening grew late, these students walked me across campus to my car, and as I drove away I couldn't help but think how rarely I had engaged the lost in such a manner. This was where I first recognized what it truly means to be missional, and by God's grace I determined then never to act in any other way again.

There was a profound benefit to both having understanding (cultural apologetics) and speaking to my audience as human beings made in the image of God and not as opponents (namely, the missional approach). If all we do is gain knowledge without understanding that this knowledge is to be used as an instrument of liberation, not condemnation, we are, as Scripture says, only resounding gongs and clanging cymbals (see 1 Corinthians 13:1)! If our motivation is anything other than love, we are nothing.

THE INFLUENTIAL "ISMS" OF OUR DAY

I will address some of the more influential ideas common to contemporary American culture in much greater detail in the subsequent chapters, but a brief summary will help the current discussion. There are the influences of modernity, those pressures and influences unique to living in a technologically advanced, industrialized modern society. In addition, there are the persistent influences of modernism — the post-Enlightenment emphasis on human reason and ingenuity as savior. In both cases, these serve to undermine our sense of the supernatural and our willingness to truly live dependent on the supernatural God. There is postmodernism, which, in one sense, exposes the futility of reliance upon human reason but goes too far by destroying the historical categories of true and false, right and wrong. Postmodernism can also go too far in undermining the traditional means of both discovering and understanding truth. In doing so, the context into which we now present the gospel story has changed radically. These changes inhibit the gospel's reception and thus we must understand this new context. Lastly, there is the all-pervading influence of consumerism, which shifts the object and aim of human life to an artificial and idealized lifestyle that can be achieved "without effort, on purchase of the appropriate commodity."[6] Consumerism is, in effect, an alternative gospel competing (rather effectively, I might add) with the true gospel.

CONFRONTING OUR MORAL ISSUES

Concerning those social influences and their underlying ideas expressed in the debates over moral and ethical questions, Christians must be equipped to recognize the logical fallacies behind false moral perspectives. Furthermore, they must subsequently affirm—in the marketplace of ideas—biblical, moral, and ethical truths in a manner that is rational, relevant, and responsible without first employing religious rhetoric and moralistic arguments. The debate over moral issues and the church's inability to preserve the biblical basis as the standard by which we make moral distinctions has contributed, more so than anything else, to the redefinition of truth in our culture. The devastating result has been the elimination of the Creator God as the absolute and exclusive source of truth in the West.

Whether it be the ideas common to a given culture or those ideas that arise out of the social debate over moral and ethical questions, both create barriers to either the reception of the gospel by nonbelievers or the *integration* of the gospel into the life of a believer. In other words, the gospel story may remain implausible in the minds of many nonbelievers, and thus they are encouraged in their unbelief. And many believers may not realize that their thinking remains largely captive to the world, and thus they fail to sanctify their theology and cultivate a comprehensive Christian life and worldview that actually changes the way they live and respond to life's challenges and opportunities. They may speak "Christianly," but they think and often act "worldly" and thus remain in captivity *to* the culture rather than being an influence *on* the culture.

To demonstrate the inextricable connection between the preservation of true ethics and morality and belief in the authority of God, consider what atheist and Yale Law School professor Arthur Leff wrote in 1979:

> If [God] does not exist, there is no metaphoric equivalent. No person, no combination of people, no document however hallowed by time,

no process, no premise, nothing as equivalent to an actual God in this central function as the unexaminable examiner of good and evil. The so-called death of God . . . seems to have effected the total elimination of any coherent, or convincing, ethical or legal system.[7]

The social acceptance of false moral perspectives has created an unprecedented culture of unbelief in America. In other words, because we (Christians) have been unable to articulate meaningful, rational, and compelling reasons for preserving biblical authority as the basis for morality, Christianity has become irrelevant in shaping the moral consensus. It naturally follows that when Christianity, Scripture, and Jesus Christ Himself are perceived as irrelevant in defining moral values, Christianity, Scripture, and Jesus would ultimately be perceived as irrelevant in the way of offering any valid explanation of anything, including reality, meaning, and purpose. If God's revelation no longer plays a central role in defining right from wrong—something that affects us on a daily basis—then why would anyone seek answers to life's larger questions from Jesus or the Bible?

THE LOSS OF THE CHRISTIAN WORLDVIEW

Our apparent inability to discern, articulate, and effectively defend biblical moral perspectives is the direct result of our lacking a comprehensive philosophy of life that is grounded in Scripture and reflected in a Christian life and worldview. According to a recent national survey by the Barna Research Group, only 4 percent of American adults have a biblical worldview as the basis of their decision making.[8] The research firm said this in describing the survey results:

If Jesus Christ came to this planet as a model of how we ought to live, then our goal should be to act like Jesus. Sadly, few people consistently demonstrate the love, obedience and priorities of Jesus. The primary reason that people do not act like Jesus is because they do not think like Jesus. Behavior stems from what we think — our attitudes, beliefs, values and opinions. Although most people own a Bible and know some of its content, our research found that most Americans have little idea how to integrate core biblical principles to form a unified and meaningful response to the challenges and opportunities of life. We're often more concerned with survival amidst chaos than with experiencing truth and significance.[9]

Barna also reported that only 51 percent of the country's Protestant pastors have a biblical worldview.[10] However, the criteria Barna's survey used to define a Christian worldview were as follows:

- Believing that absolute moral truths exist and that such truth is defined by the Bible.
- Jesus Christ lived a sinless life.
- God is the all-powerful and all-knowing Creator of the universe and He still rules it today.
- Salvation is a gift from God and cannot be earned.
- Satan is real.
- A Christian has a responsibility to share his faith in Christ with other people.
- The Bible is accurate in all of its teachings.[11]

This is hardly a comprehensive biblical framework for analyzing, evaluating, and guiding one's responses to the challenges and opportunities of life. These are merely the fundamental tenets of the Christian faith, the very basics of what it means to believe as a Christian! Again, according to this survey, only 4 percent of American adults agree with these seven statements, and yet 85 percent of Americans claim to be Christian.[12] This is basic Christian orthodoxy or essential doctrine, not a worldview in the proper sense of the term. A worldview is better understood as an all-embracing life system that emanates from our fundamental conceptions of ultimate reality. What is the essential nature of the external world? Is it ordered or chaotic? In other words, does the world owe its existence to a Creator, or is it merely the product of undirected material causes resulting from time and chance? What are our conceptions regarding the essential nature of mankind? Is man inherently prone to do good, evil, or some combination thereof? What are our ideas about knowledge and what we are able to know or how we know? Is only knowledge that is empirically provable legitimate, while experience and supernatural revelation are not? What is our understanding of good and evil (or ethics), and, finally, what is the meaning of humanity's story on the earth, or the meaning of history? A Christian worldview could be better defined as a Christian philosophy of life in which men understand all of reality and nature in connection to the revealed Word of God. A Christian worldview properly understood is when men interpret the universe and everything in it under the direction of and authority of God. Our ideas of truth, beauty, and goodness all originate in God.

WHAT IS A CHRISTIAN WORLDVIEW?

When man rebelled against God, he chose to do without God in every respect. Sinful man sought then—and continues to seek—his own ideas about truth, beauty, and goodness somewhere beyond God, either directly within himself or indirectly within the universe around him. This is the condition of every mind prior to its regeneration. Every one of us is brought to the cross by His grace, with every aspect of our being in desperate need of transformation and renewal, including our minds. This is why Romans 12:2 commands us to "not conform any longer to the pattern of this world, but be transformed by the renewing of [our minds]."

Instead of continuing to interpret the universe and everything in it from within yourself or with yourself as the ultimate point of reference (and by this I am speaking about every aspect of life: politics, economics, education, vocation, science, philosophy, as well as ethics and morality), you now seek to *reinterpret* everything you have previously understood under the direction and authority of God, from His perspective exclusively. In other words, you begin to develop a comprehensive biblical philosophy of life or Christian worldview. This is key to fulfilling the instruction given in Romans 12:1: "to offer your bodies as living sacrifices, [the entirety of your being] holy and pleasing to God" and accomplishing the goal described in the latter part of verse 2: "*Then* you will be able to test and approve what God's will is—his good, pleasing and perfect will" (emphasis added).

It can be argued that one of the principal reasons for the loss of influence of Christianity in Western civilization has been, and continues to be, a lack of commitment to a renewed intellect (or mind) operating under the direction of God. This would explain why, in large part, our salt has become tasteless and our light is hidden under a bushel. Christianity, as it is largely expressed in the American church, is no longer a transforming force in culture, and the result has been an ideological shift away from the Bible as the source of truth to one in which man has become the "measure of all things."[13]

J. Gresham Machen, the early-twentieth-century theologian and defender of the Christian faith, wrote,

> *False ideas are the greatest obstacles to the reception of the gospel. We may preach with all the fervor of a reformer yet succeed only in winning a straggler here and there, if we permit the whole collective thought of the nation or of the world to be controlled by ideas which . . . prevent Christianity from being regarded as anything more than a harmless delusion. . . . So as Christians we should try to mold the thought of the world in such a way as to make the acceptance of Christianity something more than a logical absurdity. . . . What more*

pressing duty than for those who have received the mighty experience of regeneration, who, therefore, do not, like the world, neglect that whole series of vitally relevant facts which is embraced in Christian experience—what more pressing duty than for these men to make themselves masters of the thought of the world in order to make it an instrument of truth instead of error?[14]

Amen!

AMERICAN ESCHATOLOGY: PROPHETIC FULFILLMENT OR SPIRITUAL SLOTH?

Some Christians today dismiss this cultural duty under a popular and pessimistic view of the end times. They see attempts to reform society and culture as both futile and pointless or, worse, unrelated to the Christian life. While there are indeed various eschatological perspectives on which good Christians can disagree, none relieves Christians of their responsibility to be a preserving force in the world (salt) or active advocates of truth (light). This misguided understanding is just one more example of the anti-intellectualism so prevalent in the church. In my experience, it seems that many Christians have an eschatology formed more by popular fiction than serious biblical study. Additionally, in the United States we seem to suffer from a culturally myopic view of Christianity and history that is overly American-centric; thus, we tend to interpret Scripture and historical events through uniquely American eyes. The United States of America is not the central point in human history; Jesus Christ is!

To illustrate that our current cultural calamity is a uniquely Western problem and in no way indicative of global prophetic fulfillment, Mark Hutchinson, chairman of the church history department at Southern Cross College in Australia, said, "What many pundits thought was the death of the church in the 1960s through secularization of the West was really its relocation and rebirth into the rest of the world."[15] In *The Next Christendom: The Coming of Global Christianity*, Philip Jenkins, professor of history and religious studies at Penn State, wrote, "For over a century, the coming decline or disappearance of religion has been a commonplace assumption of Western thought, and church leaders have sometimes shared this pessimistic view."[16] However, Jenkins pointed out, "We are currently living through one of the transforming moments in the history of religion worldwide. . . . The era of Western Christianity has passed within our lifetimes, and the day of Southern [referring to the southern hemisphere] Christianity is dawning."[17] Professor Jenkins added that "Christians should enjoy a worldwide boom in the new century, but the vast majority of believers will be neither white nor European, nor Euro-American."[18]

A WORLDWIDE REBIRTH

The fact is, the so-called passage of Christianity in the West is over-shadowed by the extraordinary expansion of the church currently under way throughout the rest of the world. Indeed, the numbers are astonishing. Ed Vitagliano, writing for the *American Family Association Journal*, pointed out that

> in Africa in the year 1900, for example, there were approximately 10 million Christians on the entire continent. By 2000, that number had grown to 360 million. The Anglican Communion is a perfect example of this worldwide trend. Whereas in its U.S. branch — the Episcopal Church — membership has declined over the last 40 years to 2.3 million, in Uganda alone there are more than 8 million Anglican Christians.[19]

Researcher David Barrett, author of the well-respected *World Christian Encyclopedia*, told us that "Africa is gaining 8.4 million new Christians a year."[20] Vitagliano added,

> *South Korea is another example of a nation in which the growth of Christianity has been stunning. In 1920 there were only about 300,000 believers in all of Korea. But today, in South Korea alone, there are 10 to 12 million Christians—about 25% of the population. Worldwide, evangelical Christians are a thriving part of the Christian community. Yet today, 70% of evangelical Christians live outside the West.*[21]

According to David Aikman, *Time* magazine's former chief in Beijing, "China is in the process of becoming Christianized. . . . It is possible that Christians will constitute 20 to 30 percent of China's population within three decades!"[22]

Gene Edward Veith, culture critic for *World Magazine*, pointed out that "it is not modernist, liberal Christianity that is sweeping through the Southern Hemisphere but a Christianity in which the gospel is proclaimed, that believes God's Word, that refuses to conform to the world."[23] The fact is, according to the "American Religious Identity Survey" conducted by the City University of New York, "The number of adherents to Christianity [in the United States] is in significant decline while every other false religious system is experiencing unprecedented growth."[24] These facts should challenge those who abandon their responsibilities to the culture on the assumption that the apparent decline of Christian influence in America is attributable to prophetic fulfillment. In fact, it could be argued that this very same attitude has only contributed to the church's decline and lack of relevance.

The church in America is in crisis, and this crisis cannot be dismissed or simply explained away under some end-times rationale. This crisis is quite clearly the natural consequence of biblical illiteracy,

theological ignorance, doctrinal apathy, and our subsequent conformity to the spirit of this age. As a result of our intellectual neglect, our
minds do not experience genuine renewal, and therefore our ability to
discern or prove God's good, acceptable, and perfect will in all things
is greatly limited. American Christianity has simply descended into a
shallow version of its former self—a mere shadow of historic orthodox
Christianity. The words of Romans 1:28 offer a much more plausible
explanation of our current condition: "Since [the people] did not think
it worthwhile to retain the knowledge of God, [God] gave them over to
a depraved mind, to do what ought not to be done."

Not only are we doing "what ought not to be done," as evidenced
by the dramatic moral degeneration of American culture in the past
fifty years, we (the church) are obviously not doing what we *ought to
do*, as evidenced by the widespread secularization of American culture
during this same period.

OVERCOMING OUR CULTURALIZED CHRISTIANITY

My intention here is to help Christians identify, examine, and understand the varied and often unseen ideological and social forces prevalent in today's culture, forces that inhibit their ability to think biblically
about life and the world in which they live. It is my sincere belief that
many Christians do, in fact, desire a relationship with Jesus Christ
that utterly transforms their lives and empowers them in His service.
Unfortunately, more often than not they find themselves simply
propelled along by life, never experiencing the joy of the Lord, any real
sense of meaning or purpose, or even knowing what the transformed
life is supposed to look like. These brothers and sisters are captive to the
culture by various degrees and don't know it. In the following chapters,
I will explore those largely unexamined philosophical forces in contemporary life and culture, demonstrating how these forces adversely affect
our perceptions of almost everything, including Christ and what it

means to live as a Christian. By better understanding the culture in which we live, and thus becoming missional in the sense that we are immersed and engaged, I believe that the Christian church can recover its relevance and bring honor and glory to the King of kings!

CHAPTER 2

Following Christ in the Modern World: The Challenges of Modernity and Modernism

On a spring afternoon in 1929, theologian and defender of the Christian faith J. Gresham Machen shared the following words with the graduating class of Hampden-Sydney College:

> *It is a serious step, in these days, even from the worldly point of view, to become a Christian. There was a time, not so very long ago, when the faithful Christian was supported by public opinion or at least by the united opinion of the visible church. But that time has gone by. The man who today enters upon the Christian life is enlisting in a warfare against the whole current of the age.*[1]

I think we can safely say that the "whole current of the age" has very nearly succeeded in wiping away all that remains of true Christianity in America. You may think this an overly pessimistic appraisal of the matter, but consider again the state of our culture today. All remnants of our nation's Christian heritage are being systematically removed from the public square. Virtually every institution of culture—by this I mean the media and arts, education, science and medicine, business and industry, government and law, and so on—no longer is led by Christians nor reflects the biblical view of life and reality. American universities and colleges are dominated by fundamental secularists who see higher education as a platform for liberal political indoctrination. The public education system has been reduced to a mechanism for the production of standardized thinking, if it could even be called that, with an almost exclusive emphasis on vocational training rather than virtues, character building, and critical thinking. The mere mention of anything Christian, including overtly religious holidays such as Christmas and Easter, will trigger a reaction on the scale of an international incident. With the loss of thoughtful Christian influence, art and music have been reduced to their most base forms, devoid of any objective standards by which we may judge the true, the good, and the beautiful. Secular forces driving the art community have deconstructed these categories as they have been historically understood; much of popular music has degenerated into a primitive, sexualized, and bombastic praise and worship medium for hedonism.

PRIVATE BELIEF OR PUBLIC TRUTH?

Recent political elections have exalted the position that one's private beliefs should not influence public policy, meaning that religious beliefs in particular should be excluded from the public policy arena. Of course, this perspective is telling in that it confirms that most people today categorize religion as a secondary or antiquated source of knowledge; therefore, all nonreligious or modern belief systems are regarded as both rational and the primary source of "real" knowledge. Former secretary of labor Robert Reich articulated this perspective quite clearly in an article that appeared in the *New Prospect*:

The great conflict of the 21st century may be between the West and terrorism but terrorism is a tactic and not a belief. The underlying battle will be between modern civilization and anti-modernist fanatics; between those who believe in the primacy of the individual and those who believe that beings owe blind allegiance to a higher authority; between those who give priority to life in this world and those who believe that human life is no more than preparation for an existence beyond life; between those who believe that truth is revealed solely through scripture and religious dogma, and those who rely primarily on science, reason, and logic.[2]

You can see the distinction that Reich is making here: Any attempt to derive truth from a religious worldview is openly deemed irrational, a conception that has rendered the gospel implausible in the minds of many modern people. The late Lesslie Newbigin stated it this way: "From the point of view of contemporary culture, the claim that God raised Jesus from the dead is irrational. It cannot be incorporated into the existing plausibility structure."[3]

Socially speaking, the last century has seen the legitimization of abortion, sex outside of marriage, and homosexual behavior. The whole shift in sexual ethics has completely undermined God's design for the natural family to the extent that we stand on the brink of legalizing the unthinkable: marriage between persons of the same sex, a standard never before codified in the most pagan of cultures. Yet here in America, a historically Christian nation, this notion is today advancing in our public policy. While the 2004 presidential election and the defeat of same-sex marriage efforts in eleven states offered some cause for celebration, based upon closer examination of the values and beliefs of the forthcoming generation especially, I fear this celebration is temporary unless something dramatic occurs in the spiritual life of America.

The lack of influence and subsequent exclusion of Christianity from public life has resulted from and further encourages a "privatized" faith among many professing Christians today. Unfortunately, the private version of the Christian faith is no better than its public effects, or lack thereof.

WHAT DOES THE NEXT GENERATION THINK?

So what about the next generation? According to the Barna Group, 86 percent of American teens said they were Christian in 2000. Three out of five teens said they were "committed Christians." One-third (34 percent) of all teenagers described themselves as born again, a figure that has remained unchanged in several years. And more than seven out of ten teens were engaged in some church-related activity in a typical week: attending worship services, Sunday school, a church youth group, or a small group.[4] According to these figures, we should be mightily encouraged. But sadly, that is not to be the case. If we look closer at the theological and doctrinal beliefs of the next generation of professing Christians, we can clearly see that Christianity in America is in a deplorable state of decadence and decay.

According to the same research, two out of three teens (65 percent) said that the Devil, or Satan, is not a living being but is a "symbol of evil." Three out of five teens (61 percent) agreed with the statement "If a person is generally good, or does enough good things for others during their life, they will earn a place in heaven." Slightly more than half (53 percent) said that Jesus committed sins while He was on earth.[5] Thirty percent of teens believe that all religions are really praying to the same God but are just using different names for God. In total, 83 percent of teens maintain that moral truth depends on the circumstances, and only 6 percent believe that moral truth is absolute. When it comes to believing in absolute truth, only 9 percent of born-again teens stated that they believe in moral absolutes, and just 4 percent of the non–born-again teens believe that there are moral absolutes.[6] These teens reflect the popular thinking of the day in which the notion that there is a single overarching truth about God and reality is thought to be intolerant. Apparently, this relativism neither originates within nor remains exclusive to teens. Josh McDowell reported in his recent book, *The Last Christian Generation*, that "*Newsweek* and *Beliefnet* asked 1,004 Americans this question: 'Can a person who doesn't share your religious beliefs attain salvation or go to heaven?' Sixty-eight percent of evangelical Christians said yes."[7]

The forthcoming generation of Christians seems to have lost any coherent understanding of true Christianity. Of course, this loss began with their great-grandparents; they have simply inherited the spiritual legacy handed down to them, which has become more and more diluted through each subsequent generation. As a result, too many Christians no longer have a real or meaningful understanding of who God is or how they are to relate to Him. They, like the world, have set Him at a very great distance: an irrelevant being, whose influence in their daily lives and personal decisions is marginalized at best or, worse, ignored altogether. "We all, like sheep, have gone astray" (Isaiah 53:6), embracing a way that seems right to us (see Proverbs 16:25) but is ultimately focused on ourselves and not the holy, living God — the Creator of all things and Redeemer of the world. We have descended into a form of godliness (religious practice) but deny its power (see 2 Timothy 3:5). Our post-Enlightenment, modernistic minds have pushed from the realm of possibility any idea that the supernatural God still intervenes in the daily affairs of men and that God remains central to every event and every action. In reality, we trust first in the things of this world, or the "tools of modernity" (which I will explain later). The result is that we (the church) so often confirm for the unbelieving world that they are correct in saying, "God is not real" or, at the very least, "He is irrelevant."

RELYING ON HUMAN MEANS

I am reminded of Jeremiah 2:13: "My people have committed two sins: They have forsaken me, the spring of living water, and have dug their own cisterns, broken cisterns that cannot hold water." The prophet Jeremiah is using imagery those residing in Judah would have clearly understood. Israel had forgotten the God who had led them through the desert, delivering them from bondage into the fertile land of Israel, and they defiled this land with idols. Jeremiah compared Israel's actions to someone abandoning a spring of living (running) water for broken cisterns made by men. The most reliable and refreshing sources of water in Israel were her natural springs. In contrast, the most unreliable sources of water were cisterns, large pits dug into the rock and covered with plaster, used to gather available rainwater. The water from cisterns was often salty, and if the rains were below normal, a cistern was in serious danger of running out. If a cistern developed a crack, which was prone to happen, then it would not hold the water. Cisterns, in this case, were simply the Israelites' attempt to satisfy their need apart from God. So rather than depend upon the supernatural provision of the living God, they chose to trust in their own ingenuity and resources. This is the essence of modernism: a first reliance upon human reason; modernity provides the means through technology.

MY OWN CISTERNS

In the late 1990s, I was the president and CEO of a U.S. subsidiary of a large multinational German manufacturer. My employees were well aware of my faith, and I was active in my local church. I was by every account a good Christian. Then, by God's grace, I began to realize I had been treating my relationship with Christ as a component of my life whose purpose, practically speaking, was to serve me. In other words, if I did my part—went to church, talked to others about Jesus, behaved myself, and so on — then Jesus would come alongside and bless *my* life plans and goals. He would make me happy and successful. However, I came to realize that Christ was interested in being not a component of my life but the all-encompassing purpose! My life, my plans, and my goals needed to be laid at His feet, offered entirely to *His* will, regardless of what that required. I was convicted of my self-centeredness and began to ask the Lord to capture every aspect of my life for His purpose and His glory. In short order, the Lord began to unfold a series of events in my life that would prove to be His answer to this prayer.

In August of 1999, the chairman of the board appeared in my Dallas office to announce that the Munich-based parent company had decided to sell. Given the fact that the U.S. operations were still in their start-up phase, the decision was made to liquidate all U.S. holdings in order to render the company more attractive to any potential buyers. I was given six months to shut everything down and sell all of the assets. Everything that I had worked so hard to achieve over the previous four years had come to an end. But the moment he spoke those words, I knew the Lord was preparing to do something significant in my life.

As I approached the end of that six-month period, facing unemployment for the first time in my adult life, I felt secure, confident that everything would be okay. Of course, I felt secure and confident because I had money in the bank! It was then the Lord reminded me and my wife of our commitment to our church's building campaign — a three-year pledge that just happened to be coming due the very month my employment would end. A pledge that was equal to every penny we had in the bank. Up to this point, I had reasoned with the Lord, saying stupid things like, "Lord you don't understand. I need to hang on to this money in case I don't have a job." It goes without saying, the Lord so convicted me of trusting in the work of my own hands that we wrote the check, which essentially depleted our entire savings. And this is how we entered unemployment.

Over the course of the next fourteen months, we would watch as the Lord miraculously and graciously provided, meeting all of our material needs, not to excess and often at the last moment. Nonetheless, His provision was sufficient. It was at this point that I knew the Lord was calling me into vocational ministry. I did not know where or in what capacity, but the Lord had given me a burden for the church and her relationship to the culture. I shared this desire with my church and asked that they be in prayer for guidance. A friend invited me to join him and another man for breakfast. The purpose was to meet Nathan Sheets, a man who had gone through similar circumstances and was now on staff with a global church-planting and missionary ministry. We talked for about an hour when Nathan disclosed that he had initiated the meeting in hopes of recruiting me to join their ministry; but he said, "I can tell your heart lies elsewhere and not in foreign missions. Your heart is clearly for the culture here. You should speak to a friend of mine, Dan Panetti, who is working in that kind of ministry." So Nathan immediately called Dan, and he joined us thirty minutes later. Following three hours of discussion, I felt confident this was precisely where the Lord was leading me.

The next two months would involve a series of discussions with Dan and his board, culminating in an offer to join the ministry. Included in the offer was a salary. At least that's what they called it! I had had expense accounts larger than this, and yet this is where the Lord had led me. My wife and I were fully prepared to make some lifestyle changes, but I couldn't possibly support a family of five on what was being offered. I panicked. I had a crisis of faith, convincing myself that this was all a delusion on my part; the Lord wasn't calling me to do anything! I thought I must be having some sort of midlife crisis and I just needed to go get a "real" job. This burden, once so strong, I was now willing to cast aside for some earthly security.

In the midst of this crisis I received a phone call. The caller said, "This is Judge Robert Eschenburg; do you remember me?" To which I said no. The judge responded, "I was the arbitrator in a case involving you and your wife eight years ago." Eight years earlier we'd been living in San Antonio when a water pipe burst beneath our home, causing foundation damage. We filed a homeowner's claim and the insurance company refused to pay the claim, so we went to arbitration in an effort to make them honor our policy. Now Judge Eschenburg said, "Michael, I think I ruled incorrectly in your case," and I thought, *I knew that eight years ago*. But then he said, "Because I follow Jesus Christ, I want to make it up to you."

After some discussion of the details, I hung up the phone and I wept. I was so ashamed that I had so little confidence in our great God to supply my needs when I had just watched Him do so for the past fourteen months. He was so clearly calling me to follow Him by faith, yet my sinful flesh wanted something more substantive. The Lord was gracious to me, once again demonstrating that He can be trusted. I joined the ministry, which has forever altered the course and work of my life. We sold our home, traded down our cars, went down to only one car for a time, and adjusted our lifestyle accordingly. I can't say it was easy, but the Lord met every need and continues to do so to this day. This dear brother and faithful servant of God ended up sending us $21,800, which when combined with the salary offered by the ministry proved sufficient to meet our needs in that first year.

I share this to illustrate how we so often depend on the tangibles, our own resources, and in so doing we never learn to live dependent upon the Lord and rarely experience the joy that comes from witnessing the manifest power and love of God. This is one of the great tragedies in America today—and the call upon those who still know Christ as Savior and King is to stand, at all cost, against the modern current of this age with love, grace, and sound minds grounded in theological truth, doctrinal depth, and cultural relevance. We must graciously endeavor to entreat, exhort, and persuade our brothers and sisters in Christ to understand and embrace the fullness of faith in Christ and His absolute lordship in every area of their lives.

THE CHALLENGE OF A MODERN WORLD

In seeking to understand both the causes of this condition and what we, in our imperfect flesh, can do to present ourselves as vessels equipped for His good works, I have become increasingly convinced that modernism (scientific realism, which relies on human reason and ingenuity) and modernity (the post-industrialized world) can serve as subtle but formidable barriers to both the integration and acceptance of the whole gospel.

J. Gresham Machen pointed out in the early twentieth century that

> *modern culture is a mighty force; it is either helpful to the gospel or else it is a deadly enemy of the gospel. For making it helpful neither wholesale denunciation nor wholesale acceptance is in place; careful discrimination is required, and such discrimination requires intellectual effort. Here lies a supreme duty of the modern Church.*[8]

It is precisely this type of discrimination that I am encouraging. Machen added that modernism has basically produced three negative impulses that challenge the gospel:

1. A suspicion of the past that is only natural in view of the stunning advances of recent decades.
2. Skepticism about truth and a replacement of the category of *true* with the category of *useful* (pragmatism, utilitarianism); that is, the question of what works seems to be more scientifically productive.
3. The denial that the supernatural, if there is such a thing, can break into the world.[9]

I have researched, in particular, the theological chasm that is apparent among young professing evangelicals: They claim to be Christian, they point to Christian beliefs as their basis for life and living, yet their behavior is completely inconsistent with what they claim to believe—and their theology is even worse. What they lack is a comprehensive biblical framework through which they analyze, assess, and determine their response to life's challenges and opportunities.

Recently, Christian Smith, a sociologist at the University of North Carolina–Chapel Hill, conducted the largest and most detailed study to date of teenagers and religion, the results of which were recorded in his book *Soul Searching*. In trying to characterize what churchgoing kids today actually believe, Smith coined the phrase *moralistic therapeutic deism* to describe the practical belief and practice of most professing Christian teens he and his team interviewed.[10] In general, the overwhelming majority of professing Christian teenagers believe that religion merely "makes one feel good and resolves one's problems,"[11] that religion is meant to make people "feel happy,"[12] and that God created the world and has defined the moral order but is not particularly involved in the daily affairs of people except when they need help.[13] In general, very few of the teens interviewed expressed any theological or doctrinal beliefs even remotely related to historic orthodox Christianity.

They simply do not possess a view of Christianity that connects with reality. Instead, many today follow the modernistic impulse that compels them to ultimately trust first in technology, the ingenuity of man, human reason, and the false assumption that progress is perpetual and ever upward. In other words, they are practical humanists. Thus, there is no confidence in the supernatural, and they never expect nor seek the supernatural God to intervene in human affairs. Nor do they believe He will punish their unfaithfulness (see Jeremiah 5:12). As a result of modernity, we have simply lost an understanding of who God is.

Again, it is important to note that these teens have not developed their theology in isolation from their parents or even their churches. In fact, Smith argued that contrary to many contemporary critics who tend to blame postmodernism and other such things as the preeminent cause of this crisis, American youth are not "in search of an authentic faith different from that of existing adult religion, which simply isn't cutting it."[14] In fact, Smith pointed out that "the vast majority of American teenagers are *exceedingly conventional* in their religious identity and practices," adding that "U. S. teenagers seem basically content to follow the faith of their families with little questioning."[15]

It may be easier to blame the culture for the theological ignorance of Christian youth; however, their ignorance stems from the theological training, or lack thereof, they have received. It is this very ignorance, which has only worsened in each subsequent generation, that has allowed the cultural drift that now threatens to engulf this nation.

MODERNITY: THE AIR WE BREATHE

The depth of modernity, or modern civilization—with all of its attendant forces of time pressures, consumerism, careerism, family separation, technology dependence, and distractions—is so pervasive that it is scarcely distinguishable as a force often antithetical to Christianity. Our relationship to modernity is comparable to a fish that has no concept of being wet. I think Os Guinness is helpful in further defining what we mean by the term modernity. "Modernity . . . refers to the character and system of the world produced by the forces of modernization and development, centered above all on the premise that the 'top down' causation of God and the supernatural has been decisively replaced by the 'bottom up' causation of human designs and products."[16] Modernism, the philosophical cousin to modernity, is characterized by a progressive assumption that inevitably extends to include the human heart or human moral development—in other words, a utopian worldview. Modernism posits that man, through his own reason, ability, and ingenuity, can perfect himself and that human progress is perpetual and ever upward.

We are immersed in modernity to the extent that we blindly accept everything about it as true and correct and never test the times in which we live against Scripture. This condition, coupled with its modernistic (or post-Enlightenment) assumptions,[17] has placed God at a very great distance in the lives of most professing Christians, which in turn validates this same perspective in the unbelieving culture at large. God may be ignored in the secular culture, but He is largely irrelevant among too many in the so-called Christian culture. Furthermore, this condition discourages us from pursuing knowledge of "ultimate things." We just don't think about such things anymore. As the late G. K. Chesterton said, "The modern idea is that cosmic truth is so unimportant that it cannot matter what anyone says."[18] Thus, if Christianity advances in such a culture, it often does so only at a superficial level. We tend to want to put God in a category that meets these modernistic criteria that conform to how *we* think the world is and not how God has made the world and everything in it and how He wants us to live regardless of the times.

Modernity and its attendant philosophy of modernism have had a devastating impact upon the contemporary church. While postmodernism, which I will address in the next chapter, may have raised challenges to modernism as a philosophy and does offer legitimate criticism, it nonetheless can do so only within the context of modernity. Nothing challenges modernity, which is only accelerating in the wake of ever-increasing technological capability. The result is that the helpful criticisms raised by postmodernism remain largely academic and the world rolls on in the grip of modernistic thinking. We still trust in the ingenuity of man, as evidenced by the fact that we have only *increased* expectations of our government (or the enigmatic "they") to solve every human dilemma from poverty to obesity. The modernist solution to every problem is education, in a scientific rather than moral sense; any temporary deviation from the assumed entitlement of perpetual prosperity is an aberration and must be fixed. Of course, this expectation is absolute because any impediment to personal affluence is considered unnatural in America.

The modernist mantra usually begins with the phrase "If we can put a man on the moon, then . . ." Is this not the prevailing expectation in America? Simply look at the public's reaction to the devastation of Hurricane Katrina in 2005. The first reaction was one of incredulity, in the sense of *How could this happen?* Thus, we immediately began the hunt for the person responsible, as if *surely somebody somewhere could have prevented this!* The underlying expectation is that man, through his ingenuity and genius, has the ability to completely mitigate every problem, including the power of nature.

TRUSTING IN THE THINGS OF MAN

How many of us actually live by faith, even in the slightest sense? When was the last time any of us reading this book was compelled to utterly trust in the Lord for our daily bread? Do any of us stand on the brink of starvation? Do we risk our lives in the exercise of faith in Jesus Christ? Don't we often claim martyr status when we suffer social persecution, as if that is to be compared with real persecution? Honestly, don't we really trust *first* in our jobs, the power company, modern medicine, the economic establishment, civilization, the order promised by government, technology, and so forth? In other words, we're trusting in the tools of modernity. And this is what produces such great fear in us when these fail us. When was the last time we responded to a call upon our hearts to do something that seemed irrational or was contrary to normalcy in obedience to God? Don't we privately believe and ultimately live as if God no longer calls people to the same level of radical and often irrational obedience described in Hebrews 11? And therefore we no longer expect—or perhaps more accurately, no longer *want*—this kind of call, so we do not listen nor invite God to use us in so radical a way.

Modernity, in our minds, appears to have met all of our physical needs for peace and security; it has produced the standard by which we now measure everything, including our relationship to God and His interaction with us. We have convinced ourselves that God now works exclusively through "normal" channels. We think, for example, that financial provision can come only through a job, healing can come only through medicine, peace comes only through the absolute absence of stress, joy and comfort derive from possessions and modern conveniences. By no longer expecting the supernatural to intervene in our lives, we find ourselves living day-to-day mostly independent of God until something goes wrong. When our cisterns have cracked, *then* we cry out to the Lord.

Where this impact may be most damaging is in the institutional church. This may be best exemplified in some (not all) churches caught up in church growth movements and strategies, with an unhealthy reliance upon methodologies and not the Holy Spirit. Here again, Os Guinness is helpful:

> In today's convenient, climate-controlled spiritual world created by the managerial and therapeutic revolutions, nothing is easier than living apart from God. . . . Modernity creates the illusion that, when God commanded us not to live by bread alone but by every word that comes from His mouth, He was not aware of the twentieth century. The very success of modernity may undercut the authority and driving power of faith until religion becomes merely religious rhetoric or organizational growth without spiritual reality.[19]

Our reliance on the tools and resources of modernity can and often does encourage and maintain our dependence upon the things of this world, those things we have trusted in all along. Our perspective remains horizontal, focused on the world, and seldom rises to an appropriate vertical focus on God. We rarely come to experience or seek after radical dependence upon Christ. I think this condition is central to maintaining the all-too-common sacred/secular distinction among so many professing Christians.

CHURCH RELIANCE UPON THE TOOLS OF MODERNITY

Fortunately, there are others—and I believe it is a growing number—who recognize that the contemporary church in America is in desperate need of renewal. These people rightly recognize that what often passes for Christianity in America today is a mere shadow of historic faith in Jesus Christ. However, I am concerned that some Christians' efforts at renewing the church rely solely upon the very paradigm that I am addressing. These modernistic reformers seek renewal primarily through the development of measurable metrics and strategies, such as those common to business. Their arguments are too often based upon the premise that we can, through certain processes, produce spiritual growth that is both quantifiable and duplicate-able. The problem in their minds is not theological or spiritual in origin but rather a problem of leadership, methods, and strategy. The language used is often managerial in nature, appealing to paradigms, trends, and best practices. This dependence upon processes is then defended in the name of doing "all things in excellence to the glory of God," but in the process of doing this we often eliminate God Himself from the very process.

I am not in any way denouncing progress or the benefits of modern technologies. Nor am I advocating that we dress our kids like Pilgrims and start churning our own butter! Clearly, the last three hundred years have produced extraordinary advances in science, technology, and the general quality of life. The irony is that the resultant spirit of these advances that now threaten the gospel were largely fostered by and developed as a direct result of the Christian life and worldview. These advances have proven tremendously beneficial in many respects and serve to fulfill God's longstanding commandment to "subdue the earth." I applaud such creativity; Christians *should* endeavor to utilize their God-given skills to improve the human condition to the glory of God. However, we should be warned that these very things can undermine our dependence upon God. Therefore, the condition of modernity and its inherent benefits and tools demand careful and critical scrutiny so they maintain their proper place in our lives. It is Christ, and Christ alone, who should be and remain the summit of all human focus and trust.

CHAPTER 3

Postmodernism:
An Enemy or Opportunity for the Church?

Postmodernism is perhaps one of the most misunderstood and often misapplied concepts in Western culture today. It is generally reduced to nothing more than moral relativism, which it certainly reinforces. However, the scientific age, or modernism, long ago advanced moral relativism in the form of utilitarianism—that is, the question of "What works?" rather than "What is right?" But upon closer examination, postmodernism is overstated concerning its impact on the culture: Modernity (as understood in the previous chapter) remains in my mind a much more influential impulse. However, Dick Keyes, of the L'Abri Fellowship in Massachusetts, made the point that postmodernism could be compared to a flood that has receded: "While the water may be gone, the damage nonetheless remains."[1]

Postmodernism as a philosophical reality is best remembered by the political correctness that seems to have peaked in the nineties. Certainly some of this same thinking remains in its varied forms of multiculturalism and tolerance as the ultimate virtue; however, many serious thinkers believe that postmodernism is in decline in terms of being a tangible philosophical influence.

MODERNISM REFUTED

Vladimir Lenin, in his defense of brutal totalitarianism as necessary for the implementation of communism (which was the ultimate expression of humanistic modernism in government), said, "You have to break a few eggs to make an omelet." Postmodernism reacts correctly to this claim by saying, "But you never made an omelet." In other words, postmodernism rightly observes that reliance upon the tools of modernity and all of its modernistic assumptions about the nature of man and his alleged ability to perfect himself have ultimately and utterly failed. This is the essence of postmodernism with which we, as Christians, would no doubt agree; it is a critique of modernism and all of its failed assertions.

A brief survey of the twentieth century would quickly and thoroughly confirm this. Simply consider that World Wars I and II were responsible for more than 70 million deaths.[2] The Soviet Union under Josef Stalin is estimated to have killed between 34 and 49 million of its own citizens.[3] Mao Zedong is estimated to have killed or starved to death more than 63 million human beings during his twenty-six-year reign over Communist China.[4] And roughly 9 million people died during the Russian Revolution from 1917 to 1922.[5] In fact, four times as many people were killed in the twentieth century by their own governments than were killed in all the wars with other nations during the same period.[6] And the majority of these governments were founded upon these very same modernistic assumptions. *The Black Book of Communism* estimates the number of dead resulting from communism since the Russian Revolution in 1917 to be nearly 100 million.[7] It is generally understood that the twentieth century was the bloodiest in all of human history, an ironic fact given the humanistic hope (namely, modernism) that climaxed just as that period began.

But some might dismiss these as acts of national aggression or outright evil carried out by only a few moral monsters such as Hitler, Mao, and Stalin—not necessarily evidence refuting modernistic humanism. What about the hope offered by twentieth-century science in addressing many of humanity's personal and societal ills, such as disease and poverty? Ironically, one of the most devastating plagues in all of human history occurred during the influenza pandemic of 1918 to 1919, in which an estimated 20 to 40 million people died worldwide.[8] The Spanish Flu, as it was known, killed four times as many people in a single year than the bubonic plague (or "Black Death") that occurred from 1347 to 1351. Roughly 28 percent of Americans were infected with Spanish Flu, killing an estimated 675,000—almost ten times the number killed in World War I. The Spanish Flu epidemic—from which no nation or culture was immune—is cited as the most devastating epidemic in all of recorded world history.

While we have indeed succeeded in wiping out many diseases, many more continue to appear—such as AIDS, West Nile virus, SARS—as do highly resilient varieties of age-old ailments such as cholera, pneumonia, malaria, and dysentery. In fact, in the latter half of the twentieth century, almost thirty new human diseases were identified.[9] One of the contributing factors to the high death rates associated with the Spanish Flu, particularly among the Western nations, was the less-than-vigorous response to early outbreaks. Some speculate that this was due to the increased reliance upon science and technology that arose during World War I. As such, most people living with the expectation of remedy implicit in modern society remained unalarmed until it was too late.

Regarding poverty, I am afraid the news is no better, a fact often obscured by the unparalleled prosperity of American society. It has been estimated that 1.1 billion people worldwide had consumption levels less than a dollar a day and 2.7 billion lived on less than two dollars a day in 2001.[10] That is more than half of the world's population living in abject poverty! Clearly, the postmodern criticism and rejection of modernism is overwhelmingly accurate. Postmodernism challenges, on legitimate grounds, the promise of perpetual human development and social progress that is implicit in modernism.

POSTMODERNISM AS A PHILOSOPHY

As an organized philosophical ideology, "postmodernism is primarily a reinterpretation of what knowledge is and what counts as knowledge."[11] More specifically, "it represents a form of cultural relativism about such things as reality, truth, reason, value, linguistic meaning, the self and other notions."[12] While there are a number of diverse postmodern philosophers such as Friedrich Nietzsche, Martin Heidegger, and the Swiss linguist Ferdinand de Saussure, perhaps the more influential thinker in this area was the contemporary French philosopher Jacques Derrida (1930–2004). Derrida developed a deconstructive strategy of analysis that has now been applied to literature, linguistics, philosophy, law, and architecture. Derrida's approach sought to deconstruct all prior assumptions related to these categories and question the basis of all previously held perceptions. In particular, Derrida published three books in 1967 — *Speech and Phenomena*, *Of Grammatology*, and *Writing and Difference* — that introduced this deconstructive approach to reading texts in particular.

Derrida argued that with the traditional way of reading, we make a number of false assumptions about the nature of language and texts. According to Derrida, a traditional reader believes that language is capable of expressing ideas without changing them, writing is secondary to speech in the hierarchy of language, and the author of a text is regarded as the source of its meaning. Derrida's deconstructive style of reading completely subverts these assumptions and challenges the idea that a text has an unchanging, unified meaning. In other words, Derrida believed the meaning of a text was no longer to be found in the mind of the writer but rather the reader: The reader approaches a text with a variety of cultural and environmental influences that, if different from the writer's, will by necessity produce a different interpretation. So a black male under the age of twenty-five living in South Central Los Angeles would read and interpret Shakespeare, Dickens, and the Bible differently than an elderly Asian woman living in Hong Kong. To attempt to instruct either to understand the *author's* intentions and meaning would be to impose a Western mindset in the case of Shakespeare and Dickens, and a Christian perspective in the case of the Bible. There is, of course, some truth to this, but Derrida goes too far in suggesting that, as a result of these culturally influenced interpretations, there can never be any uniform understanding of the writer's original intention. Thus, according to Derrida, we are each left with our own interpretation, and *that* interpretation then becomes the *true meaning*. Therefore, there is no single truth or meaning but rather an infinite number of truths and meanings. This is where postmodernism derives its reputation as the cause of all things relativistic, as it ultimately posits that "any claim is only true relative to the beliefs or valuations of an individual that accepts it."[13]

However, Derrida's conclusions remain academic and simply untrue. While there are certainly social, cultural, and ethnic factors that influence our perceptions, it does not mean we are utterly unable to transcend their influence in order to understand the author's perspective and, thus, his or her original meaning. Isn't this precisely the way we study Scripture, for example? It is essential to first understand to whom and in what context biblical statements were made in order to grasp their true meaning. We do this all the time and are, in fact, able to understand the author or speaker's intent and meaning. That is not to say that we do not sometimes err in our interpretation, but that does not negate the possibility of any understanding altogether, as Derrida suggests. If this were so, then there would be no effective communication with anyone anywhere. There would be no way to communicate across backgrounds and cultures, leaving us isolated and confused. Yet this is obviously not the case. Effective communication takes place every day between individuals and across the globe.

DISCREDITING HISTORY

Perhaps postmodernism's most destructive impact is in its discrediting of history as a meaningful source of knowledge and values. One of the central themes of postmodern writers and philosophers is that history is written by the victors, which thus conceals their oppressive motives. This is applied in particular to Western history, which is regarded as more oppressive than any other, as evidenced by its apparent success, which came at the expense of those cultures that stood in its way, according to postmodern thinking. This inevitably results in a portrayal of Western expansion as being driven entirely by greed and avarice, while the mostly primitive peoples the settlers encountered are portrayed as innocent and untainted by such shallow virtues. This makes the postmodern suspicious of all meta-narratives—all-encompassing stories that purport to offer a true explanation of reality—such as Western history and Christianity in particular.

First, this unbalanced perspective of history is based on the false assumption that man is inherently good and his expressions of evil derive from an external influence rather than his internal nature. This, in many respects, is nothing more than a new iteration of Jean-Jacques Rousseau's "noble savage" perspective, in which he argued that man was essentially good when in the "state of nature."[14] Second, by exploiting the thread of truth that does exist in the axiom "History is written by the victors," postmoderns are able to discredit *all* of history as unreliable. But here again, postmodernism is not alone in its diminution of history. Modernism also diminishes history as a meaningful source of knowledge by its emphasis on the future. In other words, in light of such stunning modern advances in science and technology, why look to the past? Undeniably, the combined disregard of history implicit in modernism and the disbelief of history solidified by postmodernism have thoroughly undermined the historical record as a legitimate basis for defending the claims of Scripture, moral truth, and even rational reality, for that matter.

DECONSTRUCTING TRUTH

Returning to this theme of deconstruction, postmodernism as a philosophy offers no positive agenda or any coherent solution to humanity's dilemma. It only deconstructs the traditional understanding of meaning, purpose, love, beauty, moral distinctions, and truth. Postmodernism rejects all realist commitments, such as any "theory-independent or language-independent reality or truth, the notion that there is only one way the world really is, and that the basic laws of logic apply to reality."[15] In other words, postmodernism says that nothing can be objectively true because your categories of true and false, right and wrong, are all products of cultural bias or social construction. Therefore, because each of us experiences different degrees of influence from these external forces, postmodernism assumes, and it is only an assumption, there is no overarching universal truth available for discovery. While modernism placed too much confidence in human reason and the idea of rational certitude, postmodernism dismisses human reason altogether, arguing that nothing can be known with certainty. It is important to note that biblical Christianity resides somewhere in the middle of these two extremes. Rationalism and relativism have both served to undermine the gospel.

THE DISCONNECTED GENERATION

The result of all this philosophical wrangling is a generation increasingly disconnected from any tangible sense of hope, meaning, or purpose, as well as meaningful relationships. They are being raised in a world where all of these categories have been stripped of their original content and substance. Modernism provided an object of hope other than Jesus Christ, while postmodernism, though it does reveal the futility of such misplaced hope, in the end offers nothing to fill the void. There is some evidence to support this statement. In 2003, the Commission on Children at Risk was formed to "investigate empirically the social, moral and spiritual foundations of child well-being."[16] The commission included thirty-three of the nation's leading doctors, research scientists, and mental health and youth professionals representing some of the most respected institutions of higher learning in the nation, including Harvard, Yale, and Columbia. The study was led by Dr. Kathleen Kovner Kline of Dartmouth Medical School. This commission and its representatives were not a bastion of conservativism, which makes the results all that more compelling.

Among their findings, researchers reported that "at least one of every four adolescents in the U.S. is currently at serious risk of not achieving productive adulthood."[17] Additionally, the researchers reported that "about 21 percent of U.S. children ages nine to 17 have a diagnosable mental or addictive disorder associated with at least minimum impairment."[18] Several recent studies suggest "that nearly one of every ten high school students may suffer from clinical depression."[19] There is, according to the research, a serious crisis among young people today. In summary, the researchers said, "We are witnessing high and rising rates of depression, anxiety, attention deficit, conduct disorders, thoughts of suicide, and other serious mental, emotional, and behavioral problems among U.S. children and adolescents."[20]

As to the cause of this crisis, the researchers wrote, "What's causing this crisis of American childhood is a lack of connectedness."[21] They went on to define this lack of connectedness as a lack of "close connections to other people, and deep connections to moral and spiritual meaning."[22] I would suggest that this lack of connection could be largely attributable to postmodern ambivalence. What was most astonishing to me were the unanimous recommendations of the committee in saying, "For what may be the first time, a diverse group of scientists and other experts on children's health is publicly recommending that our society pay considerably more attention to young people's moral, spiritual, and religious needs."[23] Remember, this was a secular study that sought to empirically understand the apparent crisis among American youth.

THE MISSIONAL OPPORTUNITY AND CHALLENGE

Herein lies the great opportunity for the church today, because life without hope, meaning, or purpose is simply untenable for human beings made in the image of God. The escalating destruction of the personal, psychological, and spiritual well-being of young people revealed in the aforementioned study bear this out. It seems, therefore, that postmodernism exists in a very fragile state because it conflicts with the yearnings of the human heart. We are born with a God-given desire to make sense out of life and to attempt to know our purpose and the meaning of this present reality. We simply cannot survive psychologically in a state devoid of any meaning, try as we might. This innate desire on our part is why I feel postmodernism, as a philosophy, is waning so soon after its appearance in the marketplace of ideas.

The challenge, however, is in understanding the tangible effects that postmodernism has had on real people whom we are trying to reach with the gospel—these tangible effects, again, being a suspicion of the past, a rejection of all meta-narratives, and a rejection of logic as a valid tool for discovering truth, even if such a thing exists. That might explain why, in large part, the postmodern generation of professing Christians holds little interest in doctrine, because in the end they regard doctrinal claims and theological convictions as merely different interpretations or opinions, believing there is no overarching truth to be found. The same influence might be to blame for the prominent lack of interest in church history among so many professing Christians.

In further regard to religion, postmodernism assumes—without basis—a bird's-eye view, claiming that all religions are traveling up different paths on the same mountain, ultimately reaching the same destination: God, or at least each religion's conception of God. In making this claim, postmodernism (in an obvious self-contradiction) places itself in the position of an absolute truth claim regarding religion, essentially saying that all religions are ultimately false and the only absolute truth is the postmodern perspective. In this sense, it is postmodern relativism and not Christianity, contrary to Marx's charge, that is the true "opiate of the masses." This thoughtless relativism about religion encourages people to ignore life's most important questions.

UNDERMINING THE PLURALITY OF IDEAS

Postmodernism destroys healthy pluralism, which allows for different ideas, views, and perspectives and ultimately destroys such concepts as conversion. Where a healthy plurality of ideas exists, there remains the notion that some of these ideas may, in fact, be false; thus, conversion to the truth remains possible. One can, through reasoned persuasion and argument, make one's case and convert a person to embrace his or her way of seeing the matter in question. Postmodernism renders all perspectives moot and meaningless, while a healthy pluralism maintains its respect for the varied distinctions and perspectives, thereby encouraging a diverse marketplace of ideas in which these ideas can freely compete for supremacy. In essence, postmodernism, as a philosophy, is tolerant of every belief except those that make any claim to exclusive truth, such as Christianity. Of course, postmodernism's own claim that all truth is relative, and the fact that this claim is made absolutely, is not subject to challenge.

UNDERSTANDING THE NEW CULTURAL CONTEXT FOR THE GOSPEL

Given this philosophical condition, the church must realize that the psychological context in which many people now think and live — and into which we are attempting to press the gospel — has changed dramatically. This postmodern context affects how they receive what we are saying. When we approach such people with a gospel presentation *apart from any relationship*, they are immediately suspicious and will likely categorize our motives as being merely self-motivated. Postmodern people are simply not likely to receive and respond to a random tract or visitation, although that's not to say that the Holy Spirit can't work through these. However, these people have been conditioned to be suspect of *any* claims to truth.

No, the evangelical opportunity created by postmodernism lies in the resultant desire for recovering a connectedness to other people and to spiritual meaning. The weakness of postmodern assertions — that everything is relative and ultimately nothing can be true — is that this simply conflicts with both the desires of the human heart and reality itself. Our deepest desire is to be truly loved and accepted; when we long for such relationships, we know that these desires and the resulting satisfaction are good in the absolute sense. This is rooted in our profound sense of disconnectedness from God. We know we are alienated from God; thus, we search in vain to satisfy this need through countless idols and experiences, until by God's grace, His Spirit brings us to saving faith. Additionally, most people have had enough experience with failed love and rejection to know that these feelings are bad in the absolute sense as well. We know in our innermost being that these reactions are not mere perspectives resulting from social conditioning but universally true characteristics of being human.

To be loved and accepted satisfies us; being rejected hurts us deeply. Every person knows this, even the most ardent advocate of philosophical relativism. Thus, the postmodern opportunity for the gospel begins with relationship—the simple act of caring about another human being, not for what it does for us but what it does for him, for no other reason than he is valuable, being made in the image of God. When we, as Christians, earnestly endeavor to cooperate with God to meet this deepest, most fundamental need, the illusion of relativism vanishes and the God-given yearnings of the human heart are revealed. I believe that postmodernism's inevitable conclusions—that life is meaninglessness and the prospect of ever connecting to any coherent sense of meaning or purpose is futile—have only brought these yearnings closer to the surface. We must first seek to connect to the hearts of people by genuinely caring and investing in their lives before attempting to "sell" the story of Jesus. The postmodern person must *experience* the authenticity of our faith in Jesus before he will receive it. The postmodern merely demands what Scripture confirms: that our faith be authenticated by demonstrating that we love our neighbor. This is what the unbelieving world expects from the church.

Certainly, conversion is ultimately and exclusively dependent upon the work of the Holy Spirit, and I am not suggesting we should love people only as a means of creating preconditions for salvation. We should love people because Christ first loved us. We now see other people as He saw us when we were in our own rebellious state, understanding that love cannot be reduced to a mere means to an end. In being faithful to love our neighbor as ourselves, we are directly addressing one of those false pretensions spoken of in 2 Corinthians 10:5 that is keeping people from the knowledge of God, particularly in the case of the postmodern. Simply put, the postmodern generation needs more *demonstration* of the gospel and less expression apart from love. In the words of the apostle John, "Let us not love with words or tongue but with actions and in truth" (1 John 3:18). When the church in America repents of its conformity, abandons its willful ignorance of God, and lays down its life for others, like Christ did, then this nation will once again see the truth of Christ and His kingdom.

TOWARD A NEW EPISTEMOLOGY

Contrary to popular assertions, especially by Christian leaders, postmodernism is not an entirely malevolent force that is the sole cause of relativism and the undermining of absolute truth. Certainly, there are aspects of postmodern thought that have contributed to moral relativism and the abandoning of truth as a discoverable absolute. However, this is only one direction in which postmodernism can proceed. The greater opportunity for the church—and the world, for that matter—lies in the possibility that the postmodern critique of modernism can aid in the recovery of a more Christian epistemology.

The last great epistemological shift in history occurred during the Enlightenment, when the nature of knowledge was divided into two broad categories: the world of empirical facts and the world of the metaphysical, or values. Primacy was given to the world of facts, and knowledge derived from religion, philosophy, and the like was relegated to a subordinate category and has remained there ever since. The Western world's thinking shifted from the Augustinian view, in which faith was seen as the pathway to knowledge (that is, *I believe in order to understand*) to one in which now *I must understand in order to believe*. This shift in epistemology has been devastating to the church and its mission. There was no more room for mystery and the supernatural as men became convinced of their own rational certainty and the perceived ability to know all things absolutely. But this is not the biblical way of thinking. While we believe that there is indeed absolute truth, culminating in the person of Jesus Christ, we also know that our ability to fully apprehend that truth is limited. Because of sin we "see through a glass, darkly" (1 Corinthians 13:12, KJV). That is not to say that we don't know some things absolutely; it merely means we do not know *all* things with absolute certainty. This is the epistemological assumption that postmodernism challenges and, frankly, it is much closer to a biblical epistemology that proceeds from humility than the arrogance of post-Enlightenment certitude that has come to dominate Western epistemology, both in and outside of the church.

Postmodernism has its dangers in the same way the Enlightenment had its positives. Neither is absolutely good or bad. It will therefore take a wise and committed generation of Christians to guide this latest shift in epistemology toward a more humble and Christian understanding of the nature of knowledge, what we can know, and how we know. Otherwise, as with the Age of Enlightenment, the church may once again find herself overrun by the thinking of the world rather than vice versa.

CHAPTER 4

Consumerism:
Idolatry Is Alive and Well!

While there may be some who do not conform entirely to the pressures of modernity and postmodernism, there are few in America who escape the influence and subsequent captivity of consumerism. Consumerism is a ubiquitous and persistent force working in American culture that is undermining individuals, disintegrating families and communities, and sapping the church of its influence and witness.

SHIFTING THE OBJECT AND AIM OF LIFE

Consumerism is so much more than mere materialism. It is an ideology of which materialism is merely a component; it is a way of thinking that has surreptitiously become the principal basis for how many Americans perceive life and view themselves. A ubiquitous social and economic phenomenon, consumerism derives from the "systematic creation and encouragement of the _desire_ to possess material goods and personal success in ever greater amounts."[1] In his book that reflects on capitalism and Christianity, Richard John Neuhaus clarified consumerism as "living in a manner that is measured by *having* rather than *being*."[2] In other words, consumerism shifts the object of human life from achieving personhood measured by the character of one's being to achieving personhood measured by the nature of one's possessions, appearance, and social status. Ironically, the fatal flaw in communism was that it reduced people to mere factors of production and in so doing undermined the human person's creativity and ability to give to others. In much the same way, consumerism reduces people to mere objects of consumption. Consumerism could be further understood as responding to suggestive messages that those experiences once reserved for the privileged classes, the educated elite, and the truly accomplished can all be yours *without effort*, on the purchase of the appropriate commodity.[3] The net result is the creation in our minds of an idealized lifestyle that matches those suggestive messages. It is this idealized and artificial lifestyle that is then pursued as the principal means to achieving life satisfaction, happiness, and contentment—the so-called good life. All of the consumerist's creative and intellectual energy is redirected toward this goal, a goal that is, in essence, an illusion created largely by the commercial interests of corporate America and the entertainment industry.

IMAGE OVER SUBSTANCE

According to the devotees of consumerism, one of the ways the good life can be achieved is through the endless improvement of one's self-image. While there is nothing wrong with a healthy self-image, there is something inherently destructive about an image of oneself that is rooted solely in physical appearance, social status, or material success. In such a system, human persons are, in essence, reduced to objects whose value is again determined more by *having* than *being*. The explosive growth of cosmetic surgery in this country could be largely attributed to the influence of consumerism, with its inherent emphasis on perfecting the external image in order to meet the idealized life-style represented by Madison Avenue and Hollywood, the two biggest expositors of consumerist ideology.

The late John Paul II regarded consumerism as "a threat to the freedom of the human person to live according to the higher demands of love rather than to the lower pull of material desires."[4] How true. Don't we often find ourselves driven more by the pursuit of our own material desires, a sort of dog-eat-dog mentality, than by concern for the well-being of our fellow man?

UNDERMINING THE HIERARCHY OF POSSESSIONS

Christian theology clearly teaches that it is not the possession of material goods alone, or even the desire for a better life, that is sinful; rather, it is possessing (including the *desire* to possess) without regard for the appropriate hierarchy of the material possessions and resources one has and the subordination of those goods to their proper place. Material goods and resources, according to Scripture, should remain subservient to man and available to support his service to the kingdom and his neighbor. Also, it would be a mistake to assume that consumerism is the exclusive sin of the rich. Consumerism crosses all socioeconomic classes by promoting perpetual discontentment among the haves and envy among the have-nots.

SALVATION THROUGH FINANCIAL SECURITY

Consumerism also posits that this good life can be achieved through increased financial security. The consumerist believes that financial security is the only real foundation that produces contentment, stability, and freedom to enjoy life. I would add that the consumerist tends to define financial security in very different terms. The consumerist believes financial security is achieved when he possesses the financial resources to acquire all of the commodities necessary for the idealized lifestyle. This contradicts the virtues of thrift and prudence, which achieve a sense of financial security by having something to fall back on during economic hardship.

Quite often, the preeminence of security through material acquisition leads to a validation of every decision that places career choices above everything else. For example, we do not hesitate to relocate our families for the "right opportunity," often leaving extended family behind and depriving our children of the important multigenerational influence. We are the most transient society on earth. We are consumerist nomads in continual search of greener pastures, and this nomadic condition works to *dis*integrate families and communities by severing familial and community roots. Children raised in isolation from their extended families tend to lose an important sense of connection to their past as well as to a family heritage that is larger than oneself. Grandparents, for example, serve as active participants in the family's social construction of its history, which connects members to past generations, thus promoting a sense of belonging (the connectedness mentioned in the previous chapter). The sense of belonging to something larger than just ourselves also promotes consideration of other people; it conditions us for community. The absence of these ongoing familial influences contributes to the radical individualism characteristic of American culture and serves to isolate us from our families and neighbors. We seem to be a people who are always on our way to somewhere else, never content with where we are. This is evidenced by the fact that the average length of home ownership in America is approximately six years, by far the shortest duration in the world.

UNDERMINING THE FAMILY

There is yet another area affected by the pursuit of financial security as life's panacea: The barrier that once insulated family time from employment demands is eliminated. We no longer hesitate to work weekends and evenings or to travel on Sundays, for example, in order to make that Monday-morning meeting. American workers are working more hours than ever before; the growing expectation among employers is *If you want to get ahead, you'll do what needs to be done. Otherwise you lack commitment and your career here is over.* According to a study by the Economic Policy Institute, "the average hours worked by all family members is up 11 percent since 1975"[5] and according to the Bureau of Labor, "32.8 percent of all full-time employees worked on weekends and holidays."[6] In a presentation (later reprinted in the *American Journal of Sociology*) made to the American Sociological Association annual meeting in Washington DC, sociologists concluded that "since 1969 the time American parents spend with their children has declined by 22 hours per week."[7] Americans talk of family values, but evidently we no longer value family, especially if the priority of commitment to family requires financial sacrifice and career concessions. The shield that once existed between the demands of the marketplace and the obligations of family has been obliterated; the marketplace now reigns supreme. Therefore, if family and marketplace come into conflict, the family must give way and the consumerist father rationalizes that it is ultimately for the good of the family, as he believes that the highest possible contribution of paternal parenting is economic improvement and financial stability.

UNDERMINING THE CHURCH

Americans suffer spiritually and emotionally, too. Given the extraordinary time and schedule pressures imposed on families today, as well as misplaced priorities, there is less time for involvement in the community of believers. Weekly church attendance has reached an all-time low in America, at 31 percent.[8] In addition, many people who find themselves slaves to consumerism have come to realize that, despite their having achieved the consumerist-created lifestyle, it has failed to produce the promised benefits. These discontent consumerists often then will go to religion in search of meaning and purpose. Unfortunately, many are only looking to give their lifestyle meaning and purpose; they think that by integrating "a little religion" into their lives they will balance and perfect the lifestyle. Tragically, they do not realize it is not their lifestyle that is in need of salvation, it is their very souls.

In the case of religious consumerists, they tend to respond to the forces of consumerism through increased efforts to integrate the spiritual disciplines: scheduled prayer or quiet time, regular Bible study, and so on. In other words, they approach God in the same way they approach work: as a task to be fulfilled with measurable goals to be achieved. Spiritual discipline is essential to the life of every believer; however, in the case of the consumerist, spiritual activity can become one more action item on one's to-do list. The emphasis on spirituality as another discipline can also become a form of spiritual works, in which one seeks to satisfy one's obligations to God through religious activity. Rather than adding religious activities to our lives as one among many priorities, we need to discipline our appetites and desires and learn to be content with what we have and where we are in life. Jesus Christ is not to be treated as one good among many; Jesus Christ is the supreme Good and the source and summit of all life!

UNDERMINING COMMUNITY

With the increased priority given to the marketplace, there follows a decreased commitment to neighbors, community, and connections to extended family; children are displaced in pursuit of opportunities, and familial priorities become subverted to company demands. What is perhaps most disturbing is that too many Christians are compliant in this subversion of family to work by either their unquestioning participation as employees or the imposition of these same values as employers.

Reflecting upon the post-Christian landscape of the late twenti-eth century, Christian philosopher Francis Schaeffer speculated that after the "death of God" and the resulting loss of absolute truth and moral values, modern society would be left with only the two terrible values of "personal peace and personal prosperity." Schaeffer went on to say that once these values became accepted, Americans would sacri-fice everything to protect their personal peace and affluence, including their children and their grandchildren.[9] When this artificial lifestyle becomes the object and aim of life, the consumerist, quite naturally, seeks to preserve it at all costs because in his mind, it is life.

UNDERMINING VIRTUE AND CHARACTER

Furthermore, consumerism shifts the objective of human life away from cultivating virtue and character, knowing truth, and being content to an artificially constructed, idealized lifestyle that is continually rein-forced through media, entertainment, and advertising. Again, things take priority over persons and having supersedes being, and in so doing we become a superficial culture filled with distractions that inhibit introspective thought and meaningful relationships.

In commenting on the lack of introspection that inhibits mean-ingful reflection on life's most important questions, Blaise Pascal, the seventeenth-century mathematician and Christian apologist, speaking as such a man, wrote, "As I know not whence I come, neither do I know whither I am bound; all I know is that when I quit this world, I shall fall forever either into nothingness or into the hands of an angry God, without knowing which of these two states is to be for ever my lot. . . . I must after all pass my whole life without a thought of enquiring into the issue."[10] Pascal added that "nothing is so unbearable to man as to be at a standstill, without passion, business, amusement, occupation. Tis then he feels his nothingness, his foolishness, his insufficiency, his dependence, his emptiness."[11] Pascal rightly observes that the only good thing for such men, therefore, is to be so diverted by business, sport, and amusement that they stop thinking about their circumstances. This is why we so readily embrace the distractions of consumerism. Consumerism presents us with a pleasant illusion that conceals the cosmic truth of man's rebellion (sin) and subsequent alienation from God, the effects of which have infected every aspect of life and reality.

TOO MANY CHOICES

Indeed, we live in a world full of distractions, especially when one considers that the typical American is bombarded with an average of three thousand product ads per day, almost all of which present this idealized lifestyle in its varied forms, with the key to its easy acquisition being "buy this!" However, it is not necessary to buy or even want what is offered; it is the constant barrage of images depicting the perfect life that, if viewed uncritically, can inculcate the consumerist vision. Barry Schwartz, a psychologist at Swarthmore College and author of *The Paradox of Choice*, argued that "American life is flooded with too many choices. . . . The result is a society of stressed out and unsatisfied customers."[12] Of course, this dissatisfaction is rooted in the misguided pursuit of consumer goods, which, by virtue of planned obsolescence, are designed to no longer satisfy at some point in the future. Dr. David G. Myers reported in *American Psychologist* that "compared with their grandparents, today's young adults have grown up with much more affluence, slightly less happiness and much greater risk of depression and assorted social pathology. . . . Our becoming much better off over the last four decades has not been accompanied by one iota of increased subjective well-being."[13]

PERPETUALLY DISCONTENT

In an essay on Christian asceticism, Timothy Vaverek, a Catholic priest, pointed out that "consumerism creates and nourishes human desire for temporal goods and for the sense of well-being that the acquisition and possession of those goods can provide."[14] Consumerism conditions us to never be satisfied with sufficiency but to "be all that we can be through the endless development of talent and productivity."[15] Thus, we remain perpetually discontent, unable to rest in that which is good but always wanting more. Perhaps the strongest expression of this among Christians is the idea that to be content with sufficiency is to somehow settle for less, which we condemn as lazy, defeatist, and even irresponsible. Some will vigorously defend their devotion to success in this sense as "doing all things to the glory of God" or in the name of God-honoring excellence. However, they are more often driven by the consumerist-imposed belief that *if you just work hard enough, then all will be yours*—and they must not stop until they have it all!

EXCELLENCE IN ALL THINGS

There is no question that Christianity teaches strong personal responsibility and the idea of doing our very best in everything we do. However, this does not exclude our responsibilities as husbands, wives, and parents, either. Nor does this preclude our responsibilities as prophets, priests, and kings in the world. Interestingly, those who argue this line of thinking seem to always limit their efforts for excellence to the marketplace, where consumer goods, social status, and image improvement remain the focus. Ironically, the religious consumerist does not generally apply this same energy and vigor in self-sacrificing service to God or his fellow man.

The consumerist is always telling himself that if he just works harder, he will able to make time for family, leisure, and himself later.

The religious consumerist is convinced that by working harder now, he will be able to make time for God later—but fears that any slacking off of his manic pace is a failure to use God's gifts. Again, he makes God one more item on his to-do list. In doing this, God, spiritual growth, and discipleship remain collateral categories in the consumerist life and rarely rise to become what they should be: the all-encompassing focus of human life. Vaverek went on to say that "love of God has come to mean giving thanks for His gifts by maximizing productive 'self-actualization' while love of neighbor has come to mean providing them with consumer goods."[16] Contrary to the consumerist adage that says we need to be all that we can be, we simply need to be what God wants us to be.

TYRANNY OF THE URGENT

One result of consumerism is a nation of people overwhelmed by the tyranny of the urgent, watching in disbelief as one week goes into the next, then one month, then two, then three, until years have passed and that promised lifestyle still eludes them. In the end, they are left with the realization that their life amounts to nothing more than work: They have drifted apart in their relationships, their children are grown and gone, and they have waited for that elusive goal of "mission accomplished" so they could start enjoying life, only to realize that life has already passed them by. In living this way, we are living less than we were designed to; in the meantime, our focus remains in all the wrong areas. The Christian consumerists' lives are little different from the world; their lack of countercultural living validates the unbelieving world's rejection of the gospel. Unbelievers think, *Christians don't live any different than I do, so how can this Jesus be real if He doesn't make any difference in their lives?* As Christians we are to resist worldliness and completely reorient our goals, priorities, and thinking. In essence, our lives *should* look different. Christians should serve to humanize society by demonstrating love and bringing hope to a fallen world. They should not be participating in the dehumanization — which results from reducing people to objects of consumption — that is fostered by consumerist thinking and living.

EXPORTING CONSUMERIST IDEOLOGY

It is possibly this uniquely American phenomenon that contributes to so much anti-American resentment around the world. I say uniquely American phenomenon because consumerism is a much greater problem here than anywhere else in the West. That is not to say Europeans are not affected by consumerism; however, they tend to have some natural defenses that mitigate its effects. The fact that the European countries are much more homogenous contributes to their sense of national identity and fosters a greater sense of community. This, in turn, helps preserve their commitment to familial connections and their sense of family heritage. Europeans, in general, tend to be more family-centric and more balanced in their approach to work and play. Although Europeans have numerous problems resulting from radical secularization, family separation, increased work hours, and manic lifestyles are not as large an issue as here in America.

America used to export missionaries in unparalleled number and, fortunately, still do to a large extent, but more and more we are exporting consumerist ideology — an ideology that is ultimately at odds with Christianity. My missionary friends tell me this paradox of American ideological export only adds to their challenges. In the wake of globalization, American corporations now see the world only in terms of potential markets and consumers. More and more we are telling impoverished peoples in Third World countries that they, too, can have a better life through the acquisition of the right soft drinks, clothing, and sneakers. This is powerfully reinforced through the export of Hollywood films, which, according to movie critic Michael

Medved, now receive more than 70 percent of their revenue from countries outside the United States.[17] The message of consumerism, coupled with the sexualized messages all too common to Hollywood, doesn't make for the best representation of American ideals and, by association, Christianity.

We have already demonstrated our willingness to separate trade policy from human rights policy in order to gain potential market opportunities, as in the case of China. This might be one reason why more and more nations consider us so hypocritical: We think we're "good" and that everyone should have what we have. However, when we turn a blind eye to human suffering and oppression because we are more concerned about economic opportunities, we surrender the moral high ground. Again, things rise above people, and compassion is subverted by profit. If American Christians want the world to take seriously the claims of Christ, then we must work to advance policies, both foreign and domestic, that prioritize people and moral good over economic desires. This applies to both governmental policies as well as the individual and corporate practices of the church. Specifically regarding the church, evangelicals remain the most generous in terms of charitable giving in America; however, those numbers have nonetheless been declining.[18] Furthermore, only 8 percent of professing Christians indicate that they give 10 percent of their income in the form of a tithe to their church.[19] What is perhaps most revealing related to the priorities given to money within the body of Christ in America is the fact that those making the least amount of money gave more to the church as a percentage than those with higher incomes. The disparity is significant. Among those making less than $20,000 annually, 8 percent tithed a full 10 percent of their income, while only 1 percent of those making $75,000 to $99,999 gave the 10 percent tithe.[20] Blessed are the poor indeed!

The point I am making is not an argument for tithing but rather that our tithing patterns demonstrate the priority we have given to our money, which is often allocated to our lifestyle in the form of consumer debt before it is consecrated to God or helping others. The fact is, our lifestyles are often such that we have borrowed what we have not earned to buy what we cannot afford and thus live enslaved to our creditors. Because we have prioritized the consumerist vision as the aim and object of our lives, we simply don't have anything left over to give to God and others.

BREAKING FREE OF CONSUMERIST THINKING

I hasten to add that I do not write this as one who is above and therefore immune to the pull of consumerism. Quite the contrary. As a former corporate CEO, I confess that I, too, was once very much in the grip of consumerist thinking. I deceived myself into thinking that if I did *my part* (that is, lived the faithful Christian life), then the Lord would do *His part*, which was to go along with my carefully considered life plans and objectives and favor me with His blessing. In other words, I was seeking divine approval of my consumerist lifestyle. It was not until I realized, by His grace, that Jesus Christ came to be not a component of my life but rather its all-encompassing *purpose* and Lord. Christ calls us to subordinate our lives, goals, and plans to His lordship, to be willing to accept His will no matter what might come. How often are our prayers related to our material needs versus our character needs? Certainly we are to ask the Lord for our "daily bread," but the priority should be our conformation to the image of Christ, "who, being in very nature God, did not consider equality with God something to be grasped, but made himself nothing. . . . He humbled himself and became obedient to death—even death on a cross!" (Philippians 2:6-8). Consumerism, by its very nature, opposes this self-emptying humility to which all Christians are called.

I believe the first step toward breaking free from the grip of consumerism begins with the simple recognition that this ideal is, in fact, a tangible philosophy that pervades our culture. Following this recognition, we must begin to think critically in response to the many forms and messages of consumerism, learning to filter these through the biblical understanding of life and its relationship to material goods. This recognition alone will go a long way in undermining the power and influence the messages of consumerism put forth.

Nor am I naïve about the enormous challenges associated with breaking out of the grip of consumerism. We need to discover that our satisfaction and being are to be found entirely in Christ. In regard to me and my family, it has taken time, along with numerous practical and sometimes difficult steps, to simplify our lives. Practically, this involved downsizing homes and cars, generally reducing all of our expenses, eliminating all consumer debt and credit cards, and carefully guarding my and my family's time.

The bottom line is that we must be willing to embrace a form of Christian asceticism, or simplicity, in life. Before you panic, I am not speaking of asceticism in the same degree as a twelfth-century monk; I'm talking about pursuing simplicity in as much of our lives as possible. This includes how and on what we spend our money, time, and energy. We must seek to orient our priorities toward growing in the knowledge of and devotion to God, being content with financial sufficiency, no longer always yearning for more and borrowing to buy what we have not earned. We should prioritize devotion to our spouses and the nurture and training of our children in the admonition of the Lord. Finally, we must abandon the construction of self that is rooted in the thoughts of others and instead establish our ideas of self in the imitation of Christ and His character.

The Christian life compels us to respond to God's love by imitating the self-emptying love of Christ daily. Again, Timothy Vaverek is helpful in prescribing a threefold Christian response to the lure of consumerism. Here he summarized a sound biblical approach:

Through self-denial the Christian turns away from the inessential desires of his will and his flesh, being content with God's will for his life. Through prayer he seeks deeper communion with God and the grace to persevere in the narrow path of self-sacrificial love. Through works of mercy and charity the Christian not only shares material goods with others, he pours himself out on their behalf.[21]

It is only when we Christians abandon the lure of the world presented by the empty promises of the consumerist message and unreservedly commit ourselves to the higher call of Christ that the world will see the glory of God in and through His church.

G. K. Chesterton once observed, "The Christian ideal has not been tried and found wanting. It has been found difficult; and left untried."[22] In the case of consumerism, the Christian ideal is indeed difficult, especially when the whole current of our age combines to press us in the never-ending quest to desire, acquire, and accomplish. In the consumerist culture it is difficult to "be still, and know that [He is] God" (Psalm 46:10).

PART II

Social Ideas That Hinder Belief and
Adversely Influence the Christian
Life and Witness

CHAPTER 5

The Sexualized Culture and Its Contribution to Unbelief

In the last six years of ministry, I have encountered hundreds of men and women, young and old, whose lives have been nearly destroyed by their sexual choices—choices for which they receive overwhelming social support and encouragement from the popular culture. Their stories are truly heartbreaking. My encounters with these broken men and women became so commonplace that I determined to understand what had taken place in American culture to produce these conditions in which so many people were living in apparent contradiction to traditional sexual morality. What I discovered would dramatically impact my thinking about culture and help form the basis of my future work and ministry.

THE SEXUAL REVOLUTION

We need to understand that the sexual revolution of the 1960s was arguably one of the most significant cultural events in American history, certainly within the twentieth century. It was significant in the sense that prior to the sixties, America's moral consensus was largely derived from distinctly Christian principles and values—in essence, the Christian worldview. That is not to say that everyone in America was individually Christian; certainly that was not the case. However, whether or not a person was individually Christian, society nonetheless was ordered by and operated under a distinctly Christian understanding of reality. It could be argued that this resulted more from the residual influence of earlier Christians rather than the persistent efforts of twentieth-century Christians; nonetheless, society in general embraced these Christian principles and values.

The sexual revolution was the first open rebellion against this consensus. It was, for all intents and purposes, a declaration of war against God's revealed moral standards. The sexual revolution was the beachhead from which the final assault on God's absolute moral truth was launched. The battle to redefine sexual ethics has become the ground out of which springs the cultural rejection of moral absolutes and ultimately, I believe, Christianity in America. Unfortunately, most Christians failed to recognize what was happening at the time.

SALVATION THROUGH SEX

At the heart of the prevailing values and attitudes pertaining to sex is a false doctrine of "salvation" that believes that the imposition of sexual morality itself is the cause for much of what is wrong in the world. The naturalistic, or humanistic, worldview espouses the idea that religious and social constraints (or morality) are artificially constructed concepts that inhibit natural desires. Of course, to some extent, this is true. Moral boundaries do attempt to constrain our "natural" desires; however, the difference occurs in the false presupposition that our natural desires, because they are instinctive, are inherently good and not inherently sinful. Our passions and desires do require restraint because they are often prone to perverse and self-destructive ends. Humanity is capable of both great goodness and great evil. It is the latter capacity that the natural man ignores. This ignorance defies both biblical truth and the reality of human experience. The natural man (or secularist) has become convinced that these restraints act in a repressive manner, producing guilt, which in turn causes pathologies that are ultimately self-destructive.

What is at stake in the battle to redefine sexual ethics is the very basis of truth itself. Either truth is absolute and transcendent or it is relative and subjective, meaning that truth is individually determined. It is this new idea of truth that is significantly replacing the historic conception of truth in Western culture. This is the great deception of our age. And the engine that has driven this philosophical shift in very practical terms has been and continues to be the battle to redefine sexual ethics.

It is very much like the great reformer Martin Luther once wrote,

If I profess with the loudest voice and clearest exposition every portion of the Word of God except precisely that little point which the world and the devil are at the moment attacking, I am not confessing Christ, however boldly I may be professing Christ. Where the battle rages, there the loyalty of the soldier is proved, and to be steady on all the battle front besides, is mere flight and disgrace if he flinches at that point.[1]

THE IMPACT OF SHIFTING SEXUAL ETHICS ON TRUTH

It is the concept of truth itself that the "world and the devil" are at the moment attacking, and one of the principal battlegrounds in our generation is sexual morality. This is what I believe that the apostle Paul meant when he wrote in the first chapter of Romans that "men . . . suppress the truth by their wickedness" (verse 18).

At this point it would be appropriate to offer a brief argument for the existence of absolute or objective truth. Generally speaking, today the concept of truth falls into one of two categories, either absolute or relative. Absolute or objective truth is probably best understood by examining what it is not—that is, it is not relative. As stated by J. P. Moreland and William Lane Craig in *The Philosophical Foundations for a Christian Worldview*, "relativism posits that a claim is true relative to the beliefs or valuations of an individual or group that accepts it. According to relativism a claim is made true for those who accept it by that very act."[2] Moreland and Craig offered as example, "*The earth is flat* was true for the ancients but is false for moderns."[3] However, the mere belief by the ancients that the earth was flat, even in the absence of empirical knowledge, did not make this statement true, as reality would later prove.

Moreland and Craig went on to explain that absolute or objective truth posits that "people discover truth, not create it, and a claim is made true or false in some way or another by reality itself, totally independent of whether the claim is accepted by anyone."[4] This is clearly demonstrated in the aforementioned example. That the earth was flat was in reality false despite the fact that the consensus of the ancient world may have held to the flat-earth belief. The objective truth existed in absolute terms apart from their knowledge, awaiting discovery.

It is this conception of truth that is diminishing most prominently in the area of morality and ethics. Given this relativistic moral climate, it is incumbent upon us as Christians to speak to people from a perspective demonstrating that Christianity is not merely religion but rather objective reality that is subject to some level of apprehension by a rational mind. It is objective in the sense that the observable evidence overwhelmingly validates the moral and ethical truths of the Bible. One either lives in accordance with these moral truths, in which case one is likely to experience harmony with others and existential reality

(I would call this rational living), or one acts irrationally, lives in opposition to biblical moral truth (and reality), and is therefore likely to suffer universally true and inevitable consequences. There simply is no alternative.

Many in the contemporary church have been concentrating almost exclusively on simply *expressing* the gospel, overemphasizing gospel presentations through programmatic efforts apart from relationship, charity, and acts of mercy. Other churches have embraced an unhealthy focus on helping their members find self-actualization, happiness, and prosperity. Meanwhile, Satan has been cleverly working on changing the very concept of truth itself through modern pragmatism, postmodern skepticism, and shifting sexual ethics. As a result, the prevailing conception of truth has changed so much that people can hear and even profess acceptance of the gospel and yet experience little or no change, as evidenced by the fact that while the overwhelming majority of Americans claim to be Christian, our culture is anything but.

UNDERSTANDING TRUTH AS A PREREQUISITE TO THE GOSPEL

Francis Schaeffer wrote that "truth stands before conversion—before a man is ready to become a Christian, he must have a proper understanding of truth, whether he has fully analyzed his concept of truth or not." He went on to point out, "The phrase 'accepting Christ as savior' can mean anything. We are not saying what we mean to say unless we make completely clear that we are talking about objective truth when we say Christianity is true."[5]

Understanding truth as relative can result in a relative faith or conversion. A relativistic mind considers that there are many truths, all of which are individually determined for the primary purpose of giving the individual's life meaning or merely to help him live in peace, in a metaphysical sense. I call this the "therapeutic gospel." Under the influence of this relativism, truth is often reduced to its purely personal implications. Adherents may see truth not in overarching or authoritative terms but as something that is based on their private belief; thus, their interpretation becomes the ultimate authority. When presented with the gospel, they may conclude that Christianity as a belief system may *work* for them, so they accept Christ because this is often only what the presentation requires. This kind of faith, however, is rooted in the individual's choice to believe, not the stark reality that a person existing apart from God as a result of his or her rebellion lives in darkness and bondage for a hopeless eternity!

The latter compels men to humiliation and repentance; it is the first step in dying to ourselves and surrendering to the lordship of Jesus Christ. This is what Schaeffer meant. Otherwise, when presented to a relativistic mind, the gospel often can become a "come to Jesus and be happy" proposition, not a "call upon the name of the Lord and be saved" reality. This results in nothing more than a pragmatic prescription for personal peace and prosperity: the therapeutic gospel. It is instead about what *you* have done, not the undeserved work of Christ on your behalf. This is often nothing more than self-help wrapped in religion.

In light of so much confusion, it is essential that we begin by helping people examine their own basis of truth. Schaeffer referred to this as "pre-evangelism." To do this we must gently guide people through an examination of the foundations upon which their own beliefs rest and demonstrate the point at which their beliefs conflict with reality. The subject of sexual ethics offers an excellent arena to demonstrate that false beliefs relative to sexual morality conflict with reality. In other words, once a person violates the biblical sexual ethic, which limits sexual activity to a lifelong marital commitment, there are inevitable negative consequences.

MORALITY RESTS ON THE AUTHORITY OF CHRIST

Additionally, a relativistic concept of truth has profound implications for believers because relativism under the guise of faith makes us all too comfortable with sin. The relativistic mind tends toward a sensate or emotive faith and thus may not embrace the discipline to develop a "renewed mind," which is, according to the apostle Paul, the key to becoming a living sacrifice (see Romans 12:1-2).

Furthermore, the development of a rational understanding of our faith deepens our convictions. In the absence of a renewed mind or a rational understanding of the faith, many may embrace a few Christian beliefs or propositions but still largely think—and therefore act—like the world. This might explain why the testimony of the American church is so lackluster that the unbelieving world sees little or no evidence of the life-changing power of Jesus Christ. It is this understanding—relative to the current battle to redefine sexual ethics and its relationship to our culture's concept of truth—that the church must assert in today's culture. This is an area where we must stand firm, not strictly for the regulation of behaviors but for the preservation of truth. We cannot allow the separation of ethics and morality from the authority of Christ, upon whom all true morality ultimately rests. In doing so, we undermine His relevance and authority in the minds of men and women dominated by such a culture. Thus, this shift in sexual ethics becomes a barrier to belief in Christ.

THE ORIGINS OF THE SEXUAL REVOLUTION

The sexual revolution in America, which we associate with the hippie culture of the sixties, was not the origin of this worldview; it was merely its introduction into the mainstream psyche. In order to understand the origin of this worldview, one must go back more than a century to Sigmund Freud, who famously asserted that sexual love is the prototype of all happiness. Among other things, this definition implies that love is based ultimately on the pursuit of pleasure—a quest to satisfy the self. The Freudian philosophy of sex unwittingly legitimized a view of sexuality that was self-centered rather than mutually gratifying (or other-centered) in marriage and as a result no longer limited sex to the marriage covenant—or any relational commitment whatsoever, for that matter. This stands in direct contradiction to biblical sexuality, which is inherently other-centered and, as such, intrinsic to the exclusive relationship of a safe and secure marriage.

In addition, Freud, like many others, theorized that sexual morality was an artificial social and primarily religious construct, which repressed the natural sex drive (libido), which then produced guilt, which in turn led to psychological neurosis or mental illness.[6] In contradiction to Freud's assertions, rates of mental illness in this country have reached their highest levels in this time following the sexual revolution—a time in which people have had more so-called sexual freedom than in any other period. Freud's theory offered a significant step toward separating sex from marital intimacy and responsibility. This also served to lay the foundation for replacing the Christian basis of absolute moral truth with a subjective and relativistic basis, under the guise of naturalism. In other words, sex was merely a nature-driven urge and not a covenantal expression of the one-flesh union established by God. This concept was born out of Freud's own worldview; his contempt for Christianity was indicated by his famous statement in which he called it an illusion, a crutch, and a source of guilt and pathologies.

A STRONG SEXUAL ETHIC IS DIRECTLY RELATED TO CULTURAL SUCCESS

However, in 1934 the noted British anthropologist Joseph Daniel Unwin's research demonstrated that those cultures that held to a strong sexual ethic—in which sex was strictly restricted to the marriage relationship—were as a result more productive and therefore prospered in contrast to cultures that were "sexually free."[7] Unwin studied eighty primitive and sixteen civilized cultures spanning more than five thousand years of history and found this principle to be an indisputable fact.[8] Unwin observed that the cultural condition of any society depends upon its "social energy, which is of two kinds, mental energy and creative energy."[9] Social energy, he argued, is the collective social effort directed toward the betterment of society and the common good. Societies with high levels of social energy were inherently more expansive, which gave rise to exploration, discovery, and progress in every category of creative growth. This would include areas of culture such as science, justice, education, arts, and so on. This social energy, he concluded, was greater within those cultures that held strong marital restraints on sex and greatly diminished in cultures with more liberal sexual ethics. More specifically,

> those cultures which allowed sexual freedom do not display a high level of social energy—their energy is consumed with meeting their physical appetites—they do not think large thoughts about the physical world—they are not interested in metaphysical questions regarding life and its meaning. In these cultures, life is for now.[10]

In essence, a sexually hedonistic society is inherently less productive and lacking in social vision.

A LIBERAL SEXUAL ETHIC INEVITABLY PRODUCES CULTURAL DECLINE

Additionally, those cultures that began with a strong sexual ethic and later embraced a philosophy of sexual freedom for a period of at least three generations inevitably experienced cultural demise.[11] There is not one single example in all of human history in which these cultural patterns were not consistent with Unwin's conclusions. Civilization and social order are directly related to the ideal of marriage as perceived by a given society. When society allows the extension of sexual opportunity outside the exclusive relationship of marriage, the value of marriage is diminished. Once sex is separated from marriage, society's expectations of procreative couples are decreased. With a decreased expectation upon potential parents, the family is gradually redefined to accommodate different structures as being equal. These alternative family structures are devoid of the same societal expectations of traditional marriage, namely, commitment, fidelity, and selflessness. Once the social reinforcement to lifelong marriage and parenting are removed, history demonstrates that family dissolution and infertility rates increase, thus producing the inevitable negative impact on civilization and social order. History is replete with examples that testify to this fact. The Greek, Roman, Babylonian, and Sumerian empires are all examples of cultures that began with a strong marriage-centered monogamy and later degenerated into liberal sexual practices, which, according to the sociological and anthropological evidence, preceded their demise. Of course, our own culture has suffered enormously in the wake of the sexual revolution; the societal costs of paternal absence, divorce, and out-of-wedlock births have been staggering.

So, contrary to Freud's assertions that sexual restraint was in some way repressive and therefore counterproductive to human progress, Unwin's research demonstrated the enormous social value and positive impact of biblical sexual ethics as confirmed in history and culture. Others, such as the renowned Harvard sociologist Pitirim A. Sorokin, later confirmed these same findings. Unfortunately, the Freudian theory advanced while Unwin's research faded into relative obscurity.

MARGARET SANGER'S UTOPIA

Following on the heels of Freud came another "sexual revolutionary," Margaret Sanger, who founded the American Birth Control League in 1921 (which went on to become Planned Parenthood). Seizing this concept of sexual repression, Sanger elevated sexual freedom to a religious calling. Like Freud, she believed that the repression of sexual desires was indeed harmful, theorizing that such repression would result in negative health consequences and the inhibition of intellectual capacity. Sanger believed that sexual freedom was the instrument for ultimate human progress toward a utopian world. Sanger wrote, "Through sex, mankind may attain the great spiritual illumination which will transform the world, which will light up the only path to an earthly paradise."[12]

Sanger was also an ardent advocate of eugenics. Eugenics, a term (coined by Charles Darwin's cousin) literally meaning *good births*, is a utilitarian approach to human reproduction that deals with the improvement of hereditary qualities of a particular race or individual. In essence, eugenics represented a new approach to ethics and morality in light of evolutionary theory. If natural selection was indeed the mechanism for biological progress, as Darwin argued, then reproduction of the fittest among humans should be promoted and reproduction of the unfit should be either discouraged or prevented altogether. Thus, under evolutionary moral theory, contribution to human evolutionary progress was the highest moral good, and hindrance of evolutionary progress was morally wrong. The application of eugenics was either positive or negative. In its positive application, the unfit are simply terminated—as in infanticide, genocide, and euthanasia. This was the approach of the Nazis, who carried eugenics to its full and logical conclusion. In its negative application, the unfit are merely prevented from being—as in forced birth control and abortion. In Sanger's ideal world, birth control and abortion would provide the means by which society could promote the reproduction of the intellectual and physically fit and diminish the reproduction of what she referred to as "the lower races." Sanger argued that society must apply "a stern and rigid policy of sterilization and segregation to that grade of population whose progeny is already tainted or whose inheritance is such that objection-able traits may be transmitted to offspring."[13] Sanger, along with many in the early-twentieth-century eugenics movement, believed that the unchecked reproduction of the *unfit* was "the greatest present menace to civilization."[14]

Sanger was ultimately indicted on obscenity charges. Fearing prison, she fled to Europe, leaving her husband and three children; there she began adulterous affairs with two married men. One of these men was Henry Havelock Ellis, the famed English sex researcher and one of the earliest advocates for reforming traditional Western sexual ethics. Despite Ellis's being married to a lesbian and having sex-related disorders, his research served as a significant influence on Sanger and her followers.

ALFRED KINSEY: FATHER OF THE SEXUAL REVOLUTION

Then in 1948 and 1953, Dr. Alfred Kinsey published his monumental works on male and female sexuality. Kinsey resolved to demonstrate that Americans were far more sexually active—even deviant—than had been thought up to this time. In his report on male sexuality, Kinsey writes, "Preliminary analysis of our data indicate that only a minute fraction of one per cent of the persons who are involved in sexual behavior which is contrary to the law are ever apprehended." Kinsey went on to suggest that even if law enforcement efforts resulted in a "doubling . . . in the number of arrests on sex charges, [this would] still represent no more than a fantastically minute part of the illicit activity which takes place every day in the community."[15] This led to the general acceptance of the idea that the perceived sexual morality in America was merely an illusion. In doing this, Kinsey's research would challenge the assumption that private sexual behavior has public consequences. If this were the case, then Kinsey (and others) could argue that the government had no place in the regulation of *any* sexual activity. As such, Americans became more and more desensitized to efforts to redefine sexual mores, thinking that such reform—in the name of science—was both progressive and necessary.

BAD SCIENCE

Some have said that Kinsey's research is perhaps the most cited and least read research ever conducted. Nearly all of the report's major conclusions contradicted public health data and the personal experience of most people living at the time, yet its conclusions were broadly accepted without question. However, in the years to follow and under much closer scrutiny, the Kinsey reports would be shown to contain serious shortcomings and outright fraud in both methodology and conclusions. In 1954, the American Statistical Association (ASA) published *Statistical Problems of the Kinsey Report: A Report of the American Statistical Association Committee to Advise the National Research Council Committee for Research in Problems of Sex*, by William Cochran, Frederick Mosteller, John Tukey, and W. O. Jenkins. In reviewing the *Male* report, the authors wrote, "The present results must be regarded as subject to systematic errors of unknown magnitude due to selective sampling."[16] This suggests that Kinsey "cherry-picked" the data to support his presuppositions. William Simon, a former senior member of the Kinsey research team, admitted that "Kinsey interviewed 18,000 people and used only a quarter of the cases in his two reports."[17]

In addition, Kinsey relied heavily on interviews among inmate populations and presented these findings as being representative of the general society. When challenged by a critic on this point in 1990, Kinsey Institute director June Reinisch wrote in response, "He never used . . . from such populations as the gay community or prisons, to generalize to the general public." However, in a private letter, former Institute director and early Kinsey research assistant Paul Gebhard corrected Reinisch by saying, "This statement is incorrect. *Kinsey did mix male prison inmates in with his sample.* . . . As to generalizing to a wider population, in his first volume *Kinsey did generalize to the entire U. S. population*" (emphasis added).[18]

KINSEY'S IMPACT ON THE LAW

Despite the fact that Kinsey's research, according to the eminent law professor Charles E. Rice, was "contrived, ideologically driven, and misleading,"[19] it nonetheless provided a scientific platform for the reform of America's laws governing sexual conduct and sex crimes. Funded by a large grant from the Rockefeller Foundation, the Model Penal Code of 1955, which assists legislatures in standardizing the penal law of the United States, was completely rewritten utilizing Kinsey's research to either weaken or dismantle fifty-two sex offender laws. For example, prior to Kinsey's research, rape was a capital offense, punishable by death in nineteen states. However, following the release of Kinsey's data, which claimed that "95 percent of men were already sex offenders and most women were promiscuous—or wanted to be, the justification for tough rape, child abuse and obscenity laws was largely moot."[20] Citing Kinsey's research, the death penalty for rape was eliminated in all nineteen states. Victims became suspect, sex offenders required treatment (not incarceration), and pornography became more socially acceptable.

KINSEY'S IMPACT ON THE ACCEPTANCE OF ABORTION

This research would later have a profound effect on the acceptance of abortion. Citing Kinsey, Abraham Stone and Norman E. Himes wrote *Planned Parenthood: A Practical Guide to Birth-Control Methods* in 1965, in which they state that "88 to 95 percent of premarital conceptions were terminated by induced abortion. Of the married women in the sample, 22 percent had at least one abortion."[21] This was research collected prior to 1953! What the authors did not reveal is that the sample used by Kinsey included a large population of prostitutes and the definition of *married* was applied to any woman who had "lived with a man for more than one year."[22] This alleged research originated in a claim Kinsey made before a 1955 Planned Parenthood conference; however, no such data was ever included in either of his reports on male and female sexuality. Nonetheless, this data was repeated so often that it became fact, creating a perceived epidemic of high-risk abortions performed in dangerous "back alley" procedures. This alleged and unquestioned data would no doubt go on to influence the Supreme Court's decision in *Roe v. Wade* nearly twenty years later.

KINSEY ARGUES FOR LOWER AGE OF CONSENT

Lastly, Kinsey urged numerous state legislatures to lower the age for sexual consent to ten. This was driven by his assertion that the only real harm experienced in such relationships was the result of archaic social conditioning that, in his view, ignorantly treated sex as a moral issue. Kinsey clearly advocated the abolition of all moral judgments pertaining to sexual conduct; he regarded sex as a mere biological drive, devoid of any moral connotations. Kinsey also believed that morality was the result of cultural conditioning and, as such, led to artificial distinctions such as "right and wrong, licit and illicit, normal and abnormal, acceptable and unacceptable in our social organization."[23]

There is much more that could be said of Kinsey's influence on modern sexual attitudes and his role as the "father" of the sexual revolution. Suffice it to say, there have been very few more destructive influences upon our concept of sexuality in the twentieth century.

HUGH HEFNER AND *PLAYBOY*

Following Kinsey, two principal players proved essential in moving the philosophy of sexual revolution into the mainstream. The first was Hugh Hefner. An ardent disciple of Alfred Kinsey, Hefner launched *Playboy* magazine in December 1953. In his first issue, he wrote, "We believe . . . we are fulfilling a publishing need only slightly less important than one just taken care of by the Kinsey Report." Few people today comprehend the full impact of *Playboy* and its publisher upon the reshaping of America's sexual ethics. According to Hefner, "*Playboy* freed a generation from guilt about sex, changed some laws and helped launch a revolution or two. *Playboy* is the magazine that changed America."[24]

Hefner understood that traditional biblical values restricted sex exclusively to the marriage relationship. Thus, the first obstacle for so-called sexual freedom was the elimination of the idea that men, in particular, had to be married to enjoy the sexual relationship. The elimination of this obstacle was accomplished through *Playboy*'s campaign of carefully positioned messages telling men that marriage was a slow death, that the girl next door was really a ravenous sex fiend for the taking, and that manhood was determined by the number of sexual conquests. By promoting sex outside the relationship of marriage, the personal and social value of marriage itself was eventually reduced to an archaic institution, and, for that reason, the societal expectation of commitment to marriage diminished.

Playboy would prove instrumental in advancing no-fault divorce legislation both through the messages of the magazine as well as by financing "an army of young lawyers working to eliminate the legal protections their great-grandfathers had previously embedded in American divorce law for women and children."[25] As a result, "between 1970 and 1980, forty-eight states adopted some form of no-fault divorce law."[26] America's preeminent pornographer was shaping America's family-law policies.

THE BIRTH OF PUBLIC "SEX EDUCATION"

While Hugh Hefner was popularizing the Kinsey philosophy through the first mainstream pornographic publication in America, another notable figure was introducing the Kinsey philosophy to America's schoolchildren. In 1964, the Sexuality Information and Education Council of the United States (SIECUS) was launched at the Kinsey Institute. The former medical director of Planned Parenthood, Dr. Mary Calderone, was the cofounder, along with Wardell Pomeroy, Kinsey's former partner. Calderone would also serve as SIECUS's first president. To this day, SIECUS remains one of the most influential resources for sex education in America's public schools. It may be surprising to note that the initial grant to establish SIECUS was given by none other than *Playboy* magazine. One can only conclude that *Playboy*'s interest in educating America's children on sex would be for the furtherance of the Kinsey philosophy and the ultimate cultivation of future *Playboy* consumers. The initial SIECUS sex education curriculum board was comprised entirely of "Kinseyans," committed to Kinsey's philosophy of sexuality devoid of moral restrictions.

Kinsey's assertion that early childhood sexual activity is natural and, as such, should be encouraged in order to counter "repressive morality" served as the foundation of modern sex education curriculum. The acceptance of this idea as being scientific led to the aggressive campaign to introduce sex education under the guise of personal health ran exclusively by SIECUS. Understanding human reproduction is certainly important; however, SIECUS introduced a morally nondirective approach, which was more philosophical than biological. Under this approach, children are encouraged to make their *own* choices based on what feels right for them. Today's comprehensive sex education curriculums offer little in the way of education related to the real consequences of nonmarital sex. Our children are simply encouraged to explore the sexual wilderness without any awareness of the physical, emotional, and spiritual consequences. Three decades of "safe sex" education have failed to prevent the second-highest teen pregnancy rates in the world[27] and an epidemic of sexually transmitted disease that is among the highest within the industrialized world.[28] Quite clearly this philosophy has been an abject failure.

Dr. Calderone has been recognized as one of the most influential women of the twentieth century for her role in shaping modern sex education. Unfortunately, this description is all too accurate. She wrote in her 1981 book that "a new stage of evolution is breaking across the horizon and the task of educators is to prepare children to step into that new world. To do this, they must pry children away from old views and values, especially from biblical and other traditional forms of sexual morality—for religious laws or rules about sex were made on the basis of ignorance."[29]

As I said earlier, sex education is certainly important. However, we should be teaching our children the truth about sexuality. God created sex for His good purposes and our well-being, to be enjoyed within the exclusivity of marriage. We must equip our children with the biblical understanding of sex as good, wholesome, and sacred, along with the Christian apologetic for chaste and moral relationships. Doing so will recapture the real freedom of normal love and the true beauty of sexuality that will compel our children to reject the cheap and empty version offered to them by the world. The idea of sex as recreational instead of procreational violates the natural order established by God, resulting in devastating personal and societal consequences. It is only within the physical and emotional security of a committed marriage relationship that one can experience truly fulfilling sexual experience and sexual freedom. I must point out that God is most certainly not opposed to sex, including intense sexual pleasure and satisfaction; what God opposes is the physical and emotional abandonment of those with whom we have sex.

Scripture informs us that our struggle is not against flesh and blood only but against powers and principalities (see Ephesians 6:12). What we must understand is that these powers and principalities often manifest themselves through false ideas and philosophies. It is these ideas and not just the advocates of such that we oppose. The concern for the Christian cannot be solely in controlling behaviors but rather in preserving the truth that undergirds right moral behavior, in order to limit the impact and suffering upon individual lives and families, which concerns all of humanity.

Unfortunately, the aforementioned advocates of this worldview have succeeded in completely reshaping America's values and attitudes pertaining to sexuality. The message of sex without boundaries, sex without commitment, and sex without consequences permeates every aspect of our popular culture today. As a result, the value of marriage has been eroded, sex has been reduced to self-gratification and mere copulation, and women are dehumanized and reduced to objects of sexual fulfillment.

THE EFFECTS OF THIS FALSE WORLDVIEW

Of course, the test of any worldview comes in its ability to conform to reality. In other words, if a person were to live in exact accordance with a given worldview, would his life conflict with reality at any point or work in concert with reality? In the case of this worldview, which seeks to usher in utopia by means of removing the moral boundaries related to sex, reality condemns it as being completely false. Just consider the very real consequences that have resulted.

In 1973 Americans spent approximately 10 million dollars on pornography. By 1999 the pornography industry took in more than 10 billion dollars. This is more than all revenues generated by rock-n-roll and country music and more than America spent on Broadway productions, theater, ballet, jazz and classical music combined.[30] More recent estimates place pornography revenues in excess of 14 billion dollars.

In the wake of increased sexual opportunities beyond the exclusive bonds of marriage, the public health costs are enormous. America now leads the industrialized world in sexually transmitted disease (STDs). Over 68 million Americans are currently infected and more than 15 million new cases are reported each year.[31] In the 1960s there were two recognized STDs; today there are over twenty-five, many of which are viral and have no cure.[32] Two of those will kill you! Many people are familiar with HIV/AIDS, but fewer are familiar with the second, human papilloma virus (HPV), which is the fastest-growing STD among people under the age of twenty-five. HPV is responsible for 99.7 percent of all cervical cancer,[33] killing almost five thousand women each year and rising.[34] The STD epidemic in this country has ensued despite SIECUS's four-decade campaign for condom use instead of abstinence.

Another sad consequence of the sexual revolution has been the epidemic of unwanted teenage pregnancies. Unmarried American teenagers are more likely to become pregnant than any other teenager on earth.[35]

With the growing devaluation of women implicit in the messages of our sexualized culture, it is not surprising to note that violence against them has increased 526 percent since 1960; America has the highest-reported rape rate in the world, more than thirteen times that of Great Britain and twenty times that of Japan.[36] Coincidentally, studies demonstrate a strong correlation between the sale of pornographic materials and increased rape rates.[37]

The gratification of self above all others has been extended to include the sexual abuse of children. It is estimated that one out of three girls and one out of seven boys in this country will be sexually molested before their eighteenth birthday.[38] While the media has given tremendous attention to the recent child sex-abuse scandal within the Catholic Church, WorldNet Daily reported, "In fact, a recent, federally funded study concludes the problem of school teachers molesting students dwarfs in magnitude the clergy sex-abuse scandal that rocked the Catholic Church."[39]

As it relates to abortion, what can one say except that since 1973 there have been more than 48 million abortions performed in America![40] The fact is, if abortion had nothing to do with our selfish desire to mitigate the consequences of unbridled sexual freedom, then it would not be the issue it is in our culture.

With the destruction of traditional sexual boundaries, there naturally follows the acceptance and normalization of those sexual behaviors once thought immoral and perverse, such as homosexuality. In fact, the research of J. D. Unwin offers interesting insight into the appearance of homosexuality. Unwin observed that he was "not able to find much reliable evidence in regard to homosexuality among uncivilized people."[41] Unwin concluded that the historical evidence suggests that "homosexuality is a habit that appears in a society that has been absolutely monogamous, and is relaxing"[42] its sexual mores. In other words, homosexuality is a cultural phenomenon that results from the relaxation of sexual morality, not a latent biological behavior. I will address this in greater detail in the next chapter. It is our previous cultural rejection of traditional sexual moral boundaries that explains why today more than 51 percent of American adults polled believe homosexuality is an "acceptable lifestyle."[43]

Finally and ultimately, the natural family—the cornerstone of civilization itself—suffers the worst, producing a whole host of additional deleterious effects. Divorce rates among families with children have skyrocketed in the last four decades. In 1960 only 9 percent of all children lived in single-parent families, a figure that had changed little over the course of the twentieth century; however, by 2004 the figure had jumped to 28 percent.[44] In 1960 approximately 5 percent of all births were out of wedlock; some forty-four years later, 34 percent of all births in America were out of wedlock.[45] Between 1960 and 2004, the number of unmarried cohabiting couples in America increased by nearly 1200 percent.[46] In fact, over half of all first marriages are now preceded by living together, compared to virtually none fifty years ago.[47] Quite simply, marriage and the natural family are disappearing throughout the Western world.

These are the real and devastating consequences of a culture that chooses to violate God's moral law; history has proven time and again that such contempt for these moral truths is the inevitable path to societal self-destruction.

If we hope to impact the world for the cause of Christ, we must begin by returning to and living in obedience to God's absolute moral authority in every area of our own lives first and then be prepared to offer a rational and affirming defense of God's design for sexuality and truly human relationships. Our failure to do so thus far has not only contributed to the moral demise of our formally Christianized culture but also has undermined a proper conception of truth. This altered conception of truth, as Francis Schaeffer affirms, can serve as a formidable barrier to the reception of the gospel. This fact alone should dispel the notion that the church can remain indifferent to the moral and cultural issues of the day and continue its mission in the world.

CHAPTER 6

Homosexuality:
Thinking Critically and Acting Compassionately

Following our understanding that social and moral conditions can often integrate false philosophical foundations into our collective psyche, we need to examine what is arguably the most influential element in this area at work in our culture today: the homosexual agenda. While there is certainly a general shift in sexual ethics under way in the West, there is no more orchestrated and powerful effort to redefine the moral foundations of society than that of the homosexual agenda.

When considering the issue of homosexuality and the homosexual agenda, one is reminded of the sometimes overwhelming challenge of speaking the truth in love. While on the one hand we may be able to make clear moral distinctions related to the legitimacy of homosexual behavior, we must also keep in mind that we are addressing an issue that involves people—people made in the image of God, people upon whom we should have great compassion. Yes, homosexual behavior is a sin according to Scripture; however, it is not in some higher—and therefore exclusive—category above every other sin, one or more of which we have all been guilty.

Secondly, we must separate the individual living the homosexual lifestyle from the political movement associated with the so-called homosexual agenda, as these aspects are not necessarily one and the same. Scripture clearly commands God's people to love the individual and resist the ideology represented by the political agenda—an agenda that, in this instance, seeks to abolish God's truth in human relationships and the moral order.

In responding to the persons involved in the homosexual lifestyle, the claims of the homosexual agenda, and those who support the homosexual agenda, there are three specific aspects that require our understanding in order to offer an effective apologetic or response:

1. The myths and misconceptions of the so-called gay lifestyle
2. The objective of the homosexual agenda and how it threatens social order and the church
3. How we as Christians should respond to the homosexual issue

We need to understand the issues rationally and confront them with truth in a spirit of compassion in order to dispel the many myths surrounding homosexuality that have resulted from ideologically biased rhetoric—rhetoric that has no basis in fact and yet has succeeded in silencing any opposition.

ARE PEOPLE BORN GAY?

Let us begin by addressing the myths surrounding the origins of homosexual attractions. There has been considerable research conducted in this area, specifically as it relates to the perspective that homosexual attractions are genetically predetermined—in other words, that "homosexuals are born that way," or (more relevant to the Christian)

"God made them that way." This false assertion has proven foundational in the success of the homosexual agenda by convincing a majority of Americans that this is no longer a moral issue involving behavioral choices but rather a civil rights issue involving persons who are simply born different. In doing so, activists have succeeded in elevating so-called sexual orientation to the same category as unquestioningly inherent human characteristics, such as race and gender.

This one issue alone seems central to the current false and misleading teaching plaguing so many of our churches today. In fact, only 44 percent of persons attending mainline churches believe that homosexuality is unacceptable behavior,[1] so it is not surprising to see what has recently taken place in the Episcopal Church. Similar struggles over the ordination of practicing homosexuals and compromise on the biblical prohibitions against homosexual behavior are well under way in the Presbyterian, Lutheran, and Methodist denominations as well. And make no mistake about it: This battle will most likely come to every denomination in America based upon the prevailing perceptions of the next generation on this matter.

WHAT THE SCIENCE ACTUALLY SAYS

Given the pervasive influence of the homosexual agenda on our culture (and now even the church itself), it is absolutely essential that we know and are equipped to respond with the facts. While science is certainly not the final arbiter of truth, when applied objectively it can clearly confirm the truth. However, as we well know, science can also be manipulated to support ideological agendas.

This is certainly true in the case of homosexual behavior. In essence, the so-called science supporting the notion that homosexual behavior is an inborn and unchanging trait has been, for the most part, completely rejected within the broader scientific community. Nonetheless, gay activists and the popular media have actively promoted the genetic-and-unchangeable theory, which begs the question *Is homosexuality really an inborn and normal variant of human nature?* The answer is no, and the science appears to support this position.

There is no evidence whatsoever demonstrating that homosexual behavior is simply genetic or that people are born gay, and what few laypeople know is that none of the actual research claims that there is. Dr. William Byne, director of the Laboratory of Neuroanatomy and Morphometrics at the Mount Sinai School of Medicine and member of the editorial boards at both the *Journal of Homosexuality* and *Journal of Gay and Lesbian Psychotherapy*, confirmed that "recent studies postulate biologic factors as the primary basis for sexual orientation. However, there is no evidence at present to substantiate a biologic theory."[2] More accurately, the scientific consensus suggests that homosexual behavior is the result of a complex mix of developmental factors. Nonetheless, the born-gay assertion remains unquestioned dogma among the mainstream press, liberal elites, and gay rights advocates. Researchers at the National Association for Research and Therapy of Homosexuality emphasized that:

> *It is important to understand how this deception began and how the public has been so grossly misled. In July of 1993, the research journal* Science *published a study by Dean Hamer, claiming that there might be a gene for homosexuality, supposedly proving that homosexuality is an inborn or genetic trait. Soon afterward, National Public Radio trumpeted those findings.* Newsweek *ran the cover story, "Gay Gene?"* The Wall Street Journal *announced, "Research Points Toward a Gay Gene". . . . Of course, certain necessary qualifiers were added within those news stories. But only experts knew what those qualifiers meant.*[3]

The rest of us nonscientific types were beguiled into believing that it had been proven that homosexuals were "born that way." However, here is what serious scientists know about behavioral genetics research, as reported in *Science* magazine in 1994:

> *Time and time again, scientists have claimed that particular genes or chromosomal regions are associated with behavioral traits, only to withdraw their findings when they were not replicated. Unfortunately, says Yale's Dr. Joel Gelernter, "it's hard to come up with many" findings linking specific genes to complex human behaviors that have been replicated. . . . All were announced with great fanfare; all were greeted unskeptically in the popular press; and all are now in scientific disrepute.*[4]

There are three applicable areas of research in the study of genetics as it relates to homosexual behavior. While these may be somewhat technical in nature, it is important that we at least have a working knowledge of the scientific examination of homosexual behavior in order to refute the dubious and often misrepresented scientific claims of homosexual activists.

Pillard and Bailey's Twin Study

The first is the homosexual twin study. In 1991, psychologist Michael Bailey of Northwestern University (a self-proclaimed gay-rights advocate) and psychiatrist Richard Pillard of the Boston University School of Medicine (who is an admitted homosexual) compared sets of identical (monozygotic) male twins to fraternal (dizygotic) twins. In each set, at least one twin was homosexual. They found that, among the identical twins, 52 percent were both homosexual, as opposed to the fraternal twins, among whom only 22 percent shared a homosexual orientation. These findings led Pillard and Bailey to conclude that "the pattern rates of homosexuality . . . was consistent with substantial genetic influence."[5] However, two other genetic researchers (not psychiatrists) — one heads one of the largest genetics departments in the country, the other is at Harvard—said this of the Pillard/Bailey study: "While the authors interpreted their findings as evidence for a genetic basis for homosexuality, we think that the data in fact provides strong evidence for the influence of the environment."[6] Additionally, a study published in the *Journal of Sex Research* (which examined the Minnesota Twin Registry) reported that "for men, no significant genetic effects were found . . . for sexual orientation."[7] If homosexuality were genetic, then—according to conclusions drawn in this study—*all* of the pairs of the identical twins should have been homosexual, which was not the case.

LeVay's Brain Dissection Study

The second area of research is the 1991 brain dissection study conducted by Dr. Simon LeVay.[8] LeVay, a neuroscientist and admitted homosexual working at the Salk Institute of La Jolla, California, examined the brains of forty-one cadavers: nineteen allegedly homosexual men, sixteen allegedly heterosexual men, and six allegedly heterosexual women. I say *allegedly* because of questionable assumptions made by LeVay in regard to the sixteen heterosexual men, six of whom died from AIDS. His study focused on a group of neurons in the hypothalamus structure called the interstitial nuclei of the anterior hypothalamus, technically referred to as the INAH3. He reported this region of the brain to be larger in heterosexual men than in homosexuals. Likewise, he found it to be larger in heterosexual men than in the women he studied. For that reason, he postulated homosexuality to be inborn, the result of size variations in this group of neurons in the hypothalamus; his findings were published in *Science* in August 1991. This is the study most often quoted when people insist homosexuality has been proven to be inborn.

But let's be clear: LeVay did not prove homosexuality to be inborn because his results were not uniformly consistent. On the surface it appears *all* of LeVay's homosexual subjects had smaller INAH3s than his heterosexual ones, but in fact, three of the nineteen homosexual subjects actually had *larger* INAH3s than the heterosexuals. In addition, three of the sixteen heterosexual subjects had *smaller* INAH3s than the average homosexual subject. Thus, six of LeVay's thirty-five male subjects contradicted his own theory.

Additionally, LeVay did not necessarily measure the INAH3 properly. "The area LeVay was measuring is quite small—in fact smaller than a snowflake. His peers in the neuroscientific community cannot agree on whether the INAH3, this collection of neurons in the hypothalamus, should be measured by its size/volume or by its number of neurons."[9]

Finally, it's unclear whether brain structure affects behavior or behavior affects brain structure. Dr. Kenneth Klivington, also of the Salk Institute, points out that neurons can change in response to experience. "You could postulate," he said, "that brain change occurs throughout life, as a consequence of experience."[10] In other words, even if there is a significant difference between the brain structures of heterosexual and homosexual men, it is still unclear whether the brain structure caused their homosexual orientation and behavior, or if their homosexual behavior affected their brain structure. LeVay himself reported that "the results do not allow one to decide if the size of the INAH3 in an individual is the cause or consequence of that individual's sexual orientation."[11] In fact, one year following LeVay's study, Dr. Lewis Baxter of UCLA obtained evidence through his own research that behavioral therapy can produce changes in brain circuitry.[12] Indeed, in commenting on the brain and sexual behavior, Dr. Marc Breedlove, while conducting research at the University of California at Berkeley, demonstrated that sexual behavior can actually change brain structure. Referring to his research, Breedlove stated,

> *These findings give us proof for what we theoretically know to be the case—that sexual experience can alter the structure of the brain, just*

as genes can alter it. [I]t is possible that differences in sexual behavior cause (rather than are caused by) differences in the brain.[13]

Hamer's Gene Linkage Study

Lastly, there is the third area of research: a gene linkage study conducted in 1993 by Dr. Dean Hamer of the National Cancer Institute. Hamer studied forty pairs of nonidentical gay brothers and claimed that thirty-three of the pairs had inherited the same chromosomal variant in their DNA, thus indicating a genetic cause for homosexuality. First, like LeVay's study, Hamer's results have yet to be replicated. In fact, a later, similar study actually contradicted Hamer's conclusions: George Ebers of the University of Western Ontario examined fifty-two pairs of gay brothers and found "no evidence for a linkage of homosexuality to markers on the X-chromosome or elsewhere."[14] Ebers also, with an associate, studied four hundred families with one or more homosexual males and found "no evidence for the X-linked, mother-to-son transmission posited by Hamer." In fact, Dean Hamer himself, when asked by *Scientific American* if homosexuality was rooted solely in biology, said, "Absolutely not. From twin studies, we already know that half or more of the variability in sexual orientation is *not inherited*"[15] (emphasis added).

The National Association for Research and Therapy of Homosexuality pointed out that

> *researchers' public statements to the press are often very grand and far-reaching. But when answering the scientific community, they speak much more cautiously. In qualifying their findings, researchers often use language that reporters and laypeople frankly don't understand and simply don't qualify, such as . . . "the question of the appropriate significance level to apply to a non-Mendelian trait such as sexual orientation is problematic."*[16]

For most of us, this sounds too complex to bother translating, yet it is actually a very important statement. In layman's terms, it means it is *not possible* to know what the findings mean—*if anything*—since sexual orientation cannot possibly be inherited in the direct way eye color is.

So if homosexual behavior were simply genetic, this raises the obvious question of just how these genes get passed along. As one researcher so aptly pointed out, "genetically determined homosexuality would have become extinct long ago because of reduced reproduction."[17]

INBORN DOES NOT MEAN DIVINELY SANCTIONED

Joe Dallas is a former gay-rights activist and staff member of a metropolitan community church who now counsels men and women seeking therapy for same-sex attractions; he made the point that even if homosexuality were inborn,

> *that does not necessarily mean normal. There are a number of defects or handicaps resulting from disruptions in the genetic development, which are inborn, but we would not call them normal for that reason alone. So why should we be compelled to call homosexuality normal, even if it were inborn? Inborn tendencies towards certain behaviors do not make those behaviors moral.*[18]

Recent studies now argue that a variety of behaviors may have their basis in genetics or biology. Everything from alcoholism, obesity, violence, and adultery, according to *Time* magazine, may be in our genes. If that were the case, would we then say that these tendencies are morally acceptable because they may have their roots in our biology?

So it is with homosexuality. Whether it is inborn or acquired, it is still—like all sexual contact apart from marriage—immoral. And unlike marital acts, homosexuality defies the biological design of human sexuality. Also, Scripture teaches us that we are a fallen race, born in sin. We inherited a corrupt nature with a propensity toward sin that affects us physically and spiritually (see Psalm 51:5; Romans 5:12). We were born spiritually dead (see Ephesians 2:1-2) and physically imperfect (see 1 Corinthians 15:50-54). We cannot assume, then, that because something is inborn it is also of God. There are mental, psychological, physical, and sexual aspects of our beings that God never intended us to have. In short, "inborn" does not mean "divinely sanctioned" either.[19]

CAN HOMOSEXUALS CHANGE?

Another aspect of this question that disputes the genetic theory is the fact that many homosexuals have sought and succeeded in developing normal attractions for the opposite sex. Despite pressure from homosexual activists to suppress therapeutic efforts, there is ample evidence that change is both possible and permanent.

In reviewing the research on therapy and treatment of homosexuality, Dr. Jeffrey Satinover reported a 52 percent success rate in the treatment of unwanted homosexual attractions. Masters and Johnson, the famed sex researchers, reported a 65 percent success rate.[20] Other professionals reported success rates ranging from 30 percent to 70 percent.[21] There are many men and women who would categorize their restoration to heterosexuality as deliverance from a lifestyle that is born in pain, exists in pain, and often ends in pain. To continue in the claim that homosexuality is innate and immutable is an affront to those who desire to or have already been delivered from the gay lifestyle.

IGNORING ENVIRONMENTAL INFLUENCES

Furthermore, this position prevents us as a society from addressing the very real and sometimes dysfunctional family foundations that often drive men and women into the gay community—a community that is there to accept those who so often have been ridiculed or rejected by or suffered at the hands of those whose love they most needed. Psychiatrists William Byne and Bruce Parsons reported in the *Archives of General Psychiatry* that "it seems reasonable to suggest that the stage for future sexual orientation may be set by *experiences* during early development"[22] (emphasis added). In consideration of the prevailing political climate that embraces the exclusively genetic causation, the authors wrote, "The current trend may be to underrate the explanatory power of extant psychosocial models."[23] Daniel G. Brown, citing a plethora of research that preceded the political and cultural success of the homosexual agenda, pointed out that "there is now strong evidence and considerable agreement as to family dynamics in the development of male homosexuality."[24] Often these are men and women who, because they do not fit traditional stereotypes of gender, experience abuse and rejection. Unfortunately, now we have created a culture that, upon the earliest expression of deviation from traditional gender stereotypes, often leads people to suggest that a person must therefore be gay and may actually push him or her in the direction of homosexuality.

Tragically, a more common factor in the origins of same-sex attractions is childhood sexual abuse. A study in the *Journal of Sex and Marital Therapy* reports, "According to existing literature, gender identity confusion and gender preference are often cited as being affected by childhood sexual abuse. In this study, 46 percent of the abused men, as opposed to 12 percent of the non-abused men, defined their sexual orientation as either bisexual or homosexual."[25]

GLORIFYING THE GAY LIFESTYLE

If Hollywood and the mainstream media embarked upon a campaign to present a glorified image of prostitution—in which prostitutes lived in furnished penthouse apartments, traveled by limousine, ate in the finest restaurants, and served only a limited number of "clients," all of whom were upper-class, educated men who were merely interested in female companionship (the *Pretty Woman* version as portrayed by Julia Roberts)—droves of young women would likely flock to follow this lifestyle. However, the truth, pain, and devastation of prostitution are well known, and thus Hollywood has not embarked upon an agenda to normalize that particular lifestyle (yet).

Unfortunately, the glorified version of homosexuality is continually asserted and reaffirmed through popular culture and Hollywood. Homosexual men, in particular, are continually portrayed as hip, charming, sophisticated, and handsome, with an uncanny flair for fashion—men who are merely and naturally attracted to someone of the same sex. Their only desire, like yours and mine, is to experience a lifelong committed relationship with the partner of their choice and thus form their own kind of family. However, this caricature bears no relationship to the less pleasant realities of the homosexual lifestyle. The fact is that homosexual acts are the manifestations of a deeply perverted sexual deviancy contrary to nature—a deviancy comprised of emotional, physical, and spiritual damage.

Karla Jay and Allen Young, two homosexual researchers, published one of the largest surveys ever conducted of homosexual sex practices, *The Gay Report*. According to the study, 35 percent of respondents admitted to having had one hundred or more different sexual partners throughout their lives,[26] 18 percent admitted to having had between seven and sixty such partners in the previous month alone,[27] and 18 percent to having had three or more in the previous week.[28] Thirty-eight percent said the longest relationship they had ever had did not last longer than a year.[29] For lesbians the average relationship lasted thirty-eight months.[30] Furthermore, 77 percent of respondents had taken part in threesomes at least once, while 59 percent had taken part in orgies or group sex.[31] Thirty-eight percent had partaken in sadomasochistic practices at least once, and 23 percent had practiced urination in association with sex.[32] Twenty-four percent admitted to having been paid for sex.[33] There are additional acts described in the report that are, frankly, too offensive to include here. All in all, the research revealed that sexually perverse behavior is practiced on a much larger scale within the homosexual community. This is certainly not the lifestyle represented by the mainstream media.

Homosexual activists respond to this characterization of the homosexual lifestyle by saying that researchers "gathered their data in the mid-1970s during the height of the so-called 'bathhouse culture' when, as Andrew Sullivan noted, the homosexual subculture 'all but submerged itself in a sexualized frenzy.' That 'sexualized frenzy' ended rather abruptly when a mysterious retrovirus appeared and, in a matter of years, wiped out a whole generation of homosexual men."[34] On the surface, that argument appears to make sense, and no doubt there probably was some initial degree of restraint exercised in the early days of the AIDS epidemic. However, recent data confirms that despite more than twenty years of intensive educational and public awareness campaigns against the dangers of AIDS, the incidence of unsafe sexual practices and promiscuity within the gay community remains largely unchanged. According to a study released by the Centers for Disease Control (CDC) in 1999, "The proportion of surveyed MSM (men who have sex with men) who reported having anal sex increased from 57.6 percent . . . in 1994 to 61.2 percent in 1997. . . . The proportion reporting 'always' using condoms declined from 69.6 percent in 1994 to 60.8 percent . . . in 1997."[35]

Furthermore, contrary to the ideal of persons involved in the homosexual lifestyle searching for a lifelong committed relationship, researchers found that 43 percent of white male homosexuals had sex with five hundred or more partners and 28 percent had one thousand or more sex partners![36] Even among those same-sex couples who live in a committed relationship with one partner, the research again demonstrates a very modified monogamy. In the book *The Male Couple*, the authors reported that in a study of 156 males in homosexual relationships lasting from one to thirty-seven years,

> *only seven couples (out of 156) have a totally exclusive sexual relationship, and these men all have been together for less than five years. Stated another way, all couples with a relationship lasting more than five years have incorporated some provision for outside sexual activity in their relationships.*[37]

While the current cultural climate no longer lends itself to funding research such as that presented in *The Male Couple* (since it undermines the normalization of homosexuality), the Centers for Disease Control nonetheless recently reported that "the proportion of men having multiple sex partners . . . increased from 23.6 percent . . . in 1994 to 33.3 percent . . . in 1997. . . . The largest increase . . . reported was by respondents aged less than or equal to 25 years."[38] One could safely assume that those men under the age of twenty-five are perhaps the most educated in terms of risky sexual behavior and yet this knowledge seems to have had little or no impact on curbing behaviors inherent to the homosexual lifestyle. More recently, researchers from the University of Chicago confirmed that sexual promiscuity still remains high within the gay community. Published in 2004, a three-year study on the sexual habits of Chicago's citizens revealed that 42.9 percent of homosexual men in Chicago's Shoreland area (Chicago's gay center) have had more than sixty sexual partners, while an additional 18.4 percent have had between thirty-one and sixty partners.[39] Researchers also discovered that 55.1 percent of homosexual males in Shoreland have at least one sexually transmitted disease.[40] This most recent data would seem to contradict the claim that the "sexualized frenzy" of the 1970s ended once the HIV/AIDS epidemic emerged.

Beyond the debasing sexual practices, there are the devastating and sometimes deadly health risks associated with homosexual acts. AIDS is one disease that has certainly captured the public's attention, and according to the CDC, "homosexuals comprise the single largest exposure category."[41] However, AIDS is only one of the many diseases linked to homosexual behavior. A survey of literature in leading medical journals reveals a host of medical dangers resulting specifically from homosexual sex acts as well as the promiscuous lifestyle common to homosexual behavior. Persons involved in homosexual behavior experience a wide range of bacterial infections, including gonorrhea and syphilis. One study in New York City found that "64.3 percent of the [homosexual] men reported a history of gonorrhea and/or syphilis."[42] The heterosexual community has also experienced many of these STDs but on a significantly smaller scale. Because of the unhealthy consequences inherent in the homosexual lifestyle, life expectancy is dramatically reduced, clearly demonstrating that this lifestyle is both inconsistent with the natural biological design and devastating to those who choose to embrace it.

According to a study that appeared in the *International Journal of Epidemiology*, which examined the homosexual community in Vancouver, Canada,

In a major Canadian centre, life expectancy at age 20 years for gay and bisexual men is 8 to 20 years less than for all men. If the same pattern of mortality were to continue, we estimate that nearly half of gay and bisexual men currently aged 20 years will not reach their 65th birthday. Under even the most liberal assumptions, gay and bisexual men in this urban centre are now experiencing a life expectancy similar to that experienced by all men in Canada in the year 1871.[43]

Another unhealthy characteristic of the homosexual population is their vulnerability to drug and alcohol dependence. One study that surveyed 3,400 homosexuals found "substantially higher proportions used alcohol, marijuana, or cocaine than was the case in the general population."[44] Homosexual activists would argue that this population suffers from a higher rate of drug and alcohol problems because society will not accept their sexual orientation. However, a psychological study of nearly two thousand lesbians from all fifty states found that most (57 percent) considered money the biggest worry in their lives. The study went on to state, "Only 12 percent of respondents indicated that they were concerned about people knowing that they were lesbian."[45]

Anecdotally speaking, it seems implausible that there are a vast number of persons involved in this behavior who would honestly claim to suffer as a result of society not accepting their lifestyle, especially in the midst of a culture that seems to both embrace and celebrate homosexuality. In fact, it appears in the media as if the acceptance of homosexuality is a mark of enlightenment and moral superiority in today's culture. The aforementioned findings are but a small representation of the staggering health risks inherent in homosexual acts and prolific in the gay lifestyle. Generally speaking, the evidence overwhelmingly demonstrates the devastating physiological consequences of violating the natural biological design for human sexuality.

IS IT LOVING TO PROMOTE HARMFUL BEHAVIOR?

As caring Christians, can we remain silent or, even worse, participate in the promotion of a lifestyle that has proven itself so destructive? Endorsing homosexual behavior is not the least bit compassionate, any more than is giving drugs to those addicted to illegal narcotics. We are called to be compassionate to one another, but we are not called to celebrate behavior that is clearly self-destructive and that God calls sinful. This truth is shared not as a condemnation of homosexuals but to illustrate the depths of struggle and bondage in which these men and women live. This should be of profound concern to any follower of Jesus Christ because the gospel is for all sinners, including homosexual sinners. As Paul explained to the Corinthian church after discussing various sexual sins, "Such were some of you. But you were washed, you were sanctified, you were justified in the name of the Lord Jesus Christ and by the Spirit of our God" (1 Corinthians 6:11, ESV).

We need to understand that the opposite of homosexuality is *not* heterosexuality—it is holiness! In other words, it means sexual purity for persons of either orientation: abstinence prior to marriage, sex exclusive to marriage (one man/one woman), and faithfulness within marriage. It should also be pointed out that homosexual attractions or orientation are not sin; it is only sin when those attractions are acted upon. This is the same with heterosexual attractions prior to and outside of marriage. All of us are expected to exercise personal restraint and not give in to our passion or lust. Therefore, people who admit to struggling with same-sex attractions or any sexual temptation should *not* be condemned but rather encouraged, held accountable, and strengthened in the same way we would support anyone struggling against any other sin.

WHY WE MUST OPPOSE THE POLITICAL AGENDA

While you may agree that active homosexuality is certainly immoral and that we, as Christians, should act compassionately toward those living this lifestyle, you may still be wondering how this really affects you or the society in which you live. In other words, apart from personally exercising compassion toward the homosexual man or woman, why should you oppose the political agenda of the gay rights movement? We need to understand how the legitimization of homosexual behavior threatens the family, civilization, and ultimately the gospel.

The homosexual agenda is ultimately about the complete reordering of society—more specifically, the moral foundations of society for which Christianity provides the only true basis. As Peter Kreeft pointed out in his book *How to Win the Culture War,*

> *The longest-lasting societies in history were all highly moralistic, including the Confucian (over twenty-one hundred years), the Islamic (almost 1400 years) and the Roman (about 700 years). The longest-lasting moral order in history is that of Mosaic Law: it has structured Jewish life and then Christian life for thirty-five hundred years (though not as a continuous civil society).*[46]

The unique distinction is this: In each of these cultures, the source of moral authority was transcendent, existing outside and above themselves. The authority of the moral order was maintained by means of the conscience. The moral order could also be recognized as an objective standard confirmed in nature and the reality of human experience. It was, therefore, not subject to the whims of men, but rather men were subject to it. Now, contrast that with those societies in which the source of moral authority was not transcendent but originated within man or, more specifically, a man or a group of men within that society; these were the shortest-lived societies in history. The Third Reich lasted eleven years; the Soviet Union, which was the longest surviving of such a society, lasted only seventy-two years. In addition, because these moral orders had no transcendent source to establish and maintain their authority, they were forced to employ the power of the state. This truism is reflected in "Colson's Law," which essentially states that the more a society is governed by conscience, the less it requires outside enforcement or police. The less conscience, or self-governance, the more police will be required.[47]

Kreeft went on to say, "The fact is no society has ever yet existed that has successfully built its knowledge of morality on any basis other than religion."[48] Those that have attempted to have been some of the most oppressive regimes in all of human history. And as religion was seen as an ideological opposite of these systems, it was the natural target for oppression and ultimately elimination. Don't miss this point! This is where our nation is heading unless God's people join together and stand against it.

This oppression can already be observed relative to the homosexual agenda. Canada, for example, recently passed hate-speech legislation that makes the biblical teachings about homosexuality a violation of that country's laws. Sweden passed similar legislation last summer. In each instance, the legislation in question is aimed specifically at silencing the Christian church.

Kreeft offered important insight when he wrote,

> *The idea of America becoming totalitarian may seem absurd to most Americans, but that is because they forget that there is what de Tocqueville called a "soft totalitarianism" as well as a "hard totalitarianism." The dictatorship of what Rousseau called "the general will," that is, popular opinion, can be just as totalitarian as that of any king or tyrant, and much harder to topple, especially when manipulated by a powerful and ideologically united media.*[49]

The irony is that the advocates of the homosexual agenda clearly understand their vision and goals and, more important, that Christianity is their ideological opposite. This is a fact not yet understood by many professing Christians!

This is the threat posed by the homosexual agenda: It seeks the complete and utter abolition of the "old" objective moral order, which in America (and Western civilization) is rooted solely in Christianity, to make way for the new, which is subjective and originates from within the self-interests of persons (frankly, a very small group of persons). And just so you don't think this is mere speculation on my part, read what they themselves have said on this matter. Paula Ettlebrick, the former legal director of the Lambda Legal Defense Fund, said this:

> *Being queer is more than setting up house, sleeping with a person of the same gender, and seeking state approval for doing so.* . . . *Being queer means pushing the parameters of sex, sexuality, and family, and in the process transforming the very fabric of society.*[50]

LOVING THE SINNER IS NOT PROMOTING THE SIN

This brings me to my final and perhaps most important point. We must distinguish between the homosexual agenda and the individual trapped in the sin of homosexual behavior. If we recognize the spiritual reality in which we all live, then we understand homosexuality as merely one more "pretension that sets itself up against the knowledge of God" (2 Corinthians 10:5). In other words, it is one of those deceptions constructed by Satan to keep people from knowledge of the truth. The victims are not our enemy—*Satan* is our enemy! It is he whom we fight, and the weapon he cannot overcome is the love of Jesus Christ. It is with the overwhelming force of Christ's love that we must confront the homosexual man or woman. Where do we get this idea that the first thing we need to do is to tell him the rules and then go on to immediately inform him that he is breaking them?

This is not how we speak or act before a pagan world. Consider 1 Peter 2:12: "Live such good lives among the pagans that, though they accuse you of doing wrong, they may see your good deeds and glorify God on the day he visits us." This was written to the Christians scattered throughout the Roman Empire in Asia Minor who lived in the midst of pagan cultures. These Christians—the first- and second-century Christians—laid the foundations that would conquer the Roman Empire, not by force but by their good works through the love of Christ made manifest in the church.

It was Christians who rescued the abandoned children of Rome. It was Christians who fasted for a week, not so that God would answer their prayers but so they could save the money normally spent on food and distribute it to the poor. It was Christians who, when one plague struck the Roman Empire in the first century and another in the second, went *into* the cities at great risk to their own lives to rescue those abandoned by their families; many died as a result. It was these kinds of good works that transformed a pagan culture, and it is this kind of sacrificial love and good works that can transform *our* culture.

Do we ever intentionally determine that we will be a friend to that gay man or woman with whom we work or go to school or perhaps who lives next door? What about the gay couple who arrives at our church on a Sunday morning? Will we welcome them as lost human beings in need of God's grace? I'm not talking about admitting them as members and encouraging participation in the sacraments. The Bible makes clear that the sexually immoral person who remains unrepentant is barred from uniting with the church (see 1 Corinthians 5:5-13; 6:9; Ephesians 5:3-5). However, would we make them feel welcome, praying the Lord would use us to share His love first and then by His grace, and trusting in His timing, disciple them into truth? We should. We do not compromise truth when we genuinely care about those for whom Christ died and who are in bondage. We have been given the keys of God's grace and love in Jesus Christ that will set them free. This does not mean we simply pass out gospel tracts to these people. It means we endeavor to develop caring, compassionate relationships with all who are lost, *demonstrating* the gospel to those separated from God—including those involved in homosexual behavior.

Look at our response to the AIDS crisis of the eighties. If we had responded to the homosexual community with the same sacrificial love that our first-century brothers and sisters showed their culture, the homosexual movement might not have gained the political and cultural influence it has today. Many would have found a new life in Jesus Christ, and the world would have witnessed the extraordinary love of our Lord. Yes, we certainly must speak out against the homosexual agenda with truth, no doubt, but we must also look for ways to be the instrument of Christ's love and truth to this community. We need to demonstrate the gospel rather than simply recite trite presentations.

CHAPTER 7

Why Is Marriage Important?
The Reasonable Defense of Marriage

Marriage is far more profound than our contemporary culture would lead us to believe. It is a lifelong commitment that restrains self-centeredness, self-indulgence, and self-gratification. It is the one relationship that effectively prepares and conditions us for community. By restraining self-centeredness and promoting love of another, marriage becomes the foundation for social order. When this commitment labeled *marriage* is reduced to nothing more than a mere contract between two consenting persons, or just one option among many, it ceases to restrain our self-centered passions. Self-centeredness harms not only that relationship but also others until it spreads throughout society like ripples in a pond. Abandoning the "others before self" concept of marriage for the self-serving concept of contractual relationships between autonomous individuals makes us increasingly narcissistic. This narcissism diminishes the desire for and commitment to marriage, ultimately leading toward moral and social collapse.

Across America the institution of marriage is being assailed, reduced to nothing more than a sentimental ceremony between consenting adults, radically redefined, or simply abandoned altogether. With the long-term viability of marriage in question, one must ask if the Judeo-Christian concept of marriage is really that important. Absolutely—and perhaps there is a greater need now more than ever to understand why.

Our challenge, then, is to offer a reasonable defense of marriage that not only persuades the culture to resist redefining marriage but also encourages the culture to recommit to the strengthening of marriage as an esteemed institution in society.

MARRIAGE IS UNIQUE

The Judeo-Christian concept of marriage is as old as mankind. It serves as the very foundation of civilization itself. The marriage covenant is singularly unique in civilization. It is not simply a civil union between two people; rather, it is an emotional, physical, and spiritual union between one man and one woman. It is emotional in the sense that two people, male and female, each with different attributes, join together in life, assisting one another, nurturing and caring for one another, and affirming and guiding one another—in essence, completing the other. It is physical in the sense that marriage is procreative. Two separate biological beings blend together to create what neither can create on their own: children. And lastly, marriage is spiritual in the sense that we are made for this partnership that places the interest of the other (or *others*, in the case of children) above self—a relationship that ulti-mately mirrors God's sacrificial love toward each of us and His bride, the church.

It is this deeper understanding of marriage that we must recapture for the sake of this and future generations. We simply must persuade the culture to understand the necessity of the Judeo-Christian view of marriage to social peace and order.

Augustine wrote in the fourth century, "Peace is the tranquility that is produced by order" (*tranquillitas ordinis*). Marriage is the very cornerstone of moral and social order. History has proven time and again that no community can enjoy peace and harmony without following the true moral order, and marriage provides the only effective institution for perpetuating this order.

As detailed in chapter 5, there is irrefutable evidence to support this statement relative to marriage and its role in producing not only social order but cultural prosperity as well. Again, British anthropologist J. D. Unwin demonstrated conclusively that it is marriage's role in regulating sexual behavior specifically that proves instrumental in determining a society's condition.

THE NECESSITY OF MARRIAGE TO SEX

Marriage, sex, and social order are directly related to the strength of marriage as perceived by a given society. Diminish the exclusive value of marriage by divorcing the intrinsic relationship of sex and you ultimately diminish the social order. In other words, once a culture begins to extend sexual opportunities beyond the exclusive relationship of marriage, the societal and cultural importance of marriage is diminished. As sexual opportunities are increased, our creative and social energies are redirected toward fulfilling our ever-increasing sexual appetites. This would explain much of our present obsession with sexuality, as expressed in almost all of our contemporary creative outlets: television, movies, art, and music.

By society's accepting sex outside of marriage, the social commitment to and perception of marriage inevitably changes from its essential and necessary status to a nonessential status. For example, Rutgers University conducted one of the most comprehensive studies on the state of marriage, which was published as "The State of Our Unions, The Social Health of Marriage in America, 2002." The top reason given by men for their unwillingness to commit to marriage was "They can get sex without marriage more easily than in times past."[1] History has demonstrated that we simply cannot violate God's moral order on a cultural scale and maintain social harmony and moral stability.

SEX AND ITS PROCREATIVE POTENTIAL

In his book *The Clash of Orthodoxies*, Princeton law professor Robert P. George offered the following explanation regarding the profoundly unique relationship of sex to marriage:

> *Marriage is a two-in-one-flesh communion of persons that is consummated and actualized by acts that are reproductive in type, whether or not they are reproductive in effect (or are motivated, even in part, by a desire to reproduce). The bodily union of spouses in marital acts is the biological matrix of their marriage as a multi-level relationship: that is, a relationship that unites persons at the bodily, emotional, dispositional and spiritual levels of their being. Marriage, precisely as such a relationship, is naturally ordered to the good of procreation (and to the nurturing and education of children) as well as to the good of spousal unity, and these goods are tightly bound together.*[2]

Germain Grisez, Flynn Professor of Christian Ethics at Mount Saint Mary's College in Emmitsburg, Maryland, offered further clarification on this point:

> *Though a male and female are complete individuals with respect to other functions—for example, nutrition, sensation and locomotion—with respect to reproduction they are only potential parts of a mated pair, which is the complete organism capable of reproducing sexually. Even if the mated pair is sterile, intercourse, provided it*

is the reproductive behavior characteristic of the species, makes the copulating male and female one organism.[3]

In this sense, marriage extends far beyond a mere emotional commitment and thus remains exclusive to a male/female union, for only the male and female can achieve this reproductive principle. It is for this reason that sex is intended only within the context of the marriage covenant. Marriage is the culmination of commitment on the part of two people emotionally and psychologically prepared to raise and nurture children. Therefore, marriage is a vital civil institution representing society's interest in procreative acts and the only effective means of regulating the manner and place into which children come into being and are ultimately reared.

Marriage is not a right. It is, instead, a responsibility that serves to actually restrict the rights of the individuals involved. This restriction of rights represents society's interest in the couple's procreative potential and their parental responsibilities to their offspring. The so-called marital benefits that same-sex couples seek have been reserved for traditional families by society. They are both an incentive and reward for their commitment to lifelong fidelity and preserving the best possible environment for regulating their procreative potential and subsequent child rearing. Because same-sex couples do not possess procreative potential nor fulfill this social responsibility, they are simply not eligible for marriage and the accompanying benefits.

It is this procreative potential that makes traditional marriage singularly unique among all human relationships and is, therefore, in the interest of every civilization. These marital benefits (such as tax benefits, medical rights, and so on) are, for example, also withheld from cohabiting couples despite their procreative potential because society recognizes their refusal to fully commit to this social responsibility, and the incentive therefore remains to marry.

Some may argue that couples unable to bear children or those who take steps to prevent the conception of children are exempt from this covenantal need. Not true. Whether or not marital sex acts produce children, non-childbearing couples are nonetheless participating in the same relationship, and the societal expectations do not change in response to the presence of children or lack thereof. Marriage is marriage. The absence of children, for whatever reason, does not demean that relationship to a lesser form. Socially esteemed marriage provides civic support and incentive for the preservation of their commitment to each other. Absent this commitment, there is no foundation for integrity in any relationship, and society would become nothing more than a collection of narcissists pursuing their own welfare.

SEX IS INTRINSIC TO MARRIAGE

Marriage is designed for sex, and sex is designed for marriage. Nonmarital sex ultimately harms the individual and society. Marriage is also exclusively heterosexual in that it conforms, rather self-evidentially, to the biological design for human sexuality and fulfills the reproductive principle. While same-sex couples may enjoy an emotional bond and even engage in sexual acts, they are unable to achieve this one-flesh union because there is no biological communion such as that achieved through procreative acts. In the absence of this one-flesh union, sex becomes merely instrumental for self-satisfying pleasure and therefore falls into the same category of self-centered acts that characterize all nonmarital sex. Sex becomes recreational, not relational, only engaging the physical and, to a limited extent, the emotional. In this sense, sex outside of a marriage commitment remains largely an act of taking, not giving. This is not and cannot ever be defined as marriage.

Sex outside of marriage can never provide the emotional, physical, and spiritual safety that a socially esteemed marriage commitment offers. It is within the safety of the marriage relationship, where it is reinforced and codified by society, that true sexual freedom can be experienced; this is essential to true and fulfilling intimacy between two persons. The contemporary culture's concept of sexual freedom is simply not true. Instead, it encourages intimacy apart from trust and security, thus producing serious emotional harm. This is why more than half of all cohabiting relationships end within five years.[4] In the absence of a legitimate commitment that is socially and legally reinforced, the emotional security is simply not there and, as such, people are never free to experience intimacy as intended and designed by God.

GOD IS FOR GOOD SEX!

As Christians, we must affirm that God is not opposed to sex, even great and pleasurable sex. Rather, God opposes the abandonment of those with whom we have sex. This is why God has created and requires the lifelong commitment unique to marriage prior to having sex — for our pleasure and protection as well as the fulfillment of necessary social and familial roles and responsibilities.

Given the fact that marriage is one of only three earthly institutions (the church, the state, and the family) established by God, we, as followers of Christ, have a duty to defend this truth. However, it is the manner of our defense that may prove instrumental; we must appeal to reason and not to fear, offering the overwhelming evidential truth of traditional marriage.

THE BENEFITS OF MARRIAGE

There are a multitude of documented benefits unique to marriage. According to the eminent University of Chicago sociologist Linda Waite,

> *Married people live longer, are healthier, have fewer heart attacks and other diseases, have fewer problems with alcohol, behave in less*

risky ways, have more sex—and more satisfying sex—and become much more wealthy than single people. There was one exception to this rosy picture: cohabiting couples do have more frequent sex. But they enjoy it less.[5]

Regarding mortality, studies reveal that "mortality rates are 50 percent higher for unmarried women and 250 percent higher for unmarried men than they are for married women and men."[6] For men matched in every respect except marital status, nine out of ten married men who were alive at age 48 made it to 65; only six out of ten bachelors lived to the usual retirement age.[7]

One of the most common cultural myths relative to marriage centers around sexual satisfaction. If one were to believe the popular media, one would quickly conclude that marriage deals a death blow to exciting and frequent sex. However, all the research demonstrates just the opposite. According to a University of Chicago national sex survey, 43 percent of married men reported having sex at least twice a week, while only 1.26 percent of single men not cohabiting had sex that often.[8] Additionally, 50 percent of married men and 42 percent of married women find sex physically and emotionally satisfying, while only 39 percent of cohabiting men and 39 percent of cohabiting women do.[9]

Another overlooked benefit of marriage is that of physical security for women. Although some may want you to believe that marriage facilitates the oppression and subjugation of women, the reality is that the primary source of domestic abuse in this country is not spousal abuse; it is nonspousal abuse. According to the National Crime Victimization Survey conducted by the U.S. Department of Justice, of all violent crimes against partners that occurred between 1979 and 1987, boyfriends or ex-husbands committed 65 percent. Husbands presently living with their wives committed only 9 percent of these crimes. A redesigned study changed the statistics somewhat: 55 percent were committed by boyfriends, 31 percent by husbands, and 14 percent by ex-husbands.[10] Nonetheless, the evidence overwhelmingly demonstrates that being *unmarried* puts women at a much higher risk of domestic abuse. Rates of violence for cohabiting couples were twice as high, and the overall rates for "severe" violence was nearly five times as high when compared with married couples.[11]

Beyond any domestic living arrangements, marriage affords women greater security from all other types of physical assault. According to the research, "single women are ten times more likely to be victims of rape and three times more likely to be victims of aggravated assault."[12] This is attributable to a higher level of commitment intrinsic in marriage in which a husband generally holds his wife in higher regard, which motivated him to commit to marriage in the first place. Also, a husband more so than a "boyfriend" is integrated into his wife's family and thus accountable to in-laws as well as other extended family members. A boyfriend is, by very nature of the relationship, less permanent and thus less committed. Marriage elevates the male/female relationship to a point at which much more is at stake, and as such there is a stronger incentive among the participants to preserve the peace and promote the success of the couple's union.

COHABITATION: A POOR PREFACE TO MARRIAGE

Another common myth is that living together prior to marriage serves as an effective testing ground, increasing a couple's chances for a long-term, healthy marriage. However, four decades of sociological evidence overwhelmingly demonstrate that just the opposite is true. In fact, the evidence reveals that cohabitation not only fails to prepare couples for marriage but also contributes to decreased marital stability in the future. According to studies conducted in Canada, Sweden, and the United States, couples who cohabit prior to marriage have substantially higher divorce rates. The recorded differences range from 50 to 100 percent higher.[13] According to the research, cohabitation is associated with greater marital conflict and poorer communication;[14] cohabiters perceive a greater likelihood of divorce than couples who did not cohabit before marriage; and longer cohabitation was associated with a higher likelihood of divorce.[15] Cohabitation is *not* related to marital happiness but instead is related to low levels of marital satisfaction, high levels of marital disagreement, and marital instability.[16] The chance of a woman's marriage dissolving is, on average, nearly 80 percent higher for those who cohabited premaritally with their future spouses than for those who did not.[17] Married couples were significantly more egalitarian in their role expectations than cohabiting subjects.[18]

One possible cause for the instability inherent in cohabitation is the lack of social reinforcement for fidelity that is implicit in marriage. Research again reveals that currently cohabiting and postmarital cohabiting individuals are less committed to their present partner in regard to the possibility of sexual encounters with others outside of the current relationship.[19]

Furthermore, cohabiting couples seldom accumulate wealth in the same way married couples do. They are far more tentative about their relationship; less inclined to invest together in homes, stocks, and furniture; and more likely to do such things as keep separate bank accounts and take separate vacations.[20] And finally, the physical and sexual abuse of children is much higher in cohabiting families and stepfamilies than in married families.[21] In light of the overwhelming data, cohabitation is not only a poor preparation and substitute for marriage, it is, according to the evidence, active in undermining the couple's future prospects for marriage.

WHAT ABOUT SAME-SEX MARRIAGE?

All right, you say, so cohabitation is a poor substitute for marriage and may even undermine those marriages preceded by cohabitation.

But how does allowing persons of the same sex to marry harm the institution of marriage? This is a commonly asked question in the course of debate relative to redefining marriage to include persons of the same sex. Those in favor of allowing same-sex couples to marry base their argument solely on the emotional aspect, completely ignoring the larger aspects of procreation and the natural family. As I have indicated earlier, this is the continuation of the process that undermines marriage itself, producing deleterious effects on the children in these modified families and subsequently in the broader society.

There is some empirical evidence demonstrating that the allowance of same-sex marriage within a given culture will, in fact, harm the institution of marriage. As Dr. Stanley Kurtz, senior fellow at Stanford University's Hoover Institute, reported before the House Judiciary Committee in April of 2004, there is ample evidence in the experience of Scandinavia. Dr. Kurtz holds a PhD in social anthropology from Harvard University and is regarded as both an excellent scholar and expert in this area. Kurtz wrote,

> *The Swedes have simply drawn the final conclusion: If we've come so far without marriage, why marry at all? Our love is what matters, not a piece of paper. Why should children change that?*[22]

Indeed, Sweden's out-of-wedlock birthrate is 55 percent, Norway's is 50 percent, Iceland's is approaching 70 percent, and in Denmark 60 percent of firstborn children are born out of wedlock. And, again according to Dr. Kurtz, studies in these countries demonstrate that unmarried families break up at a rate two to three times that of married couples. This has only exacerbated the welfare state that is unparalleled in Scandinavia. No western nation has a higher percentage of public employees, public expenditures, or higher tax rates than Sweden, for example.[23]

All of the Scandinavian countries mentioned embraced *de facto* same-sex marriage, beginning with Denmark in 1989. The out-of-wedlock birthrates given earlier experienced their most dramatic increases in the decade following the acceptance of same-sex marriage in these countries. The separation of marriage from parenting was already increasing, as it is here; gay marriage only widened the separation. "In Scandinavia, gay marriage has driven home the message that marriage itself is outdated, and that virtually any family form, including out-of-wedlock parenthood, is acceptable."[24]

Dr. Kurtz offered the following further insight into the connection between cohabitation, rising out-of-wedlock birthrates, and same-sex marriage:

> *British demographer Kathleen Kiernan . . . divides the continent into three zones. The Nordic countries are the leaders in cohabitation and out-of-wedlock births. They are followed by a middle group that includes the Netherlands, Belgium, Great Britain, and Germany. . . . North American rates of cohabitation and out-of-wedlock birth put the United States and Canada into this middle group. Most resistant to cohabitation, family dissolution, and out-of-wedlock births are the southern European countries of Portugal, Italy, and Greece. . . . These three groupings closely track the movement for gay marriage. In the late eighties and early nineties, gay marriage came to the Nordic countries, where the out-of-wedlock birthrate was already high. Ten years later, out-of-wedlock birthrates have risen significantly in the middle group of nations. Not coincidentally, nearly every country in that middle group has recently either legalized some form of gay marriage, or is seriously considering doing so. Only in the group with low out-of-wedlock birthrates has the gay marriage movement achieved relatively little success.[25]*

Kurtz concluded by saying, "This suggests that gay marriage is both an effect and a cause of the increasing separation between marriage and parenthood. As rising out-of-wedlock birthrates disassociate heterosexual marriage from parenting, gay marriage becomes conceivable."[26]

This begs the question *If marriage is only about a relationship between two people and is not intrinsically connected to procreation and parenthood, why shouldn't same-sex couples be allowed to marry?* It quite naturally follows that "once marriage is redefined to accommodate same-sex couples, that change cannot help but lock in and reinforce the very cultural separation between marriage, procreation and parenthood that makes gay marriage conceivable to begin with."[27]

Lastly, gay marriage has not strengthened the institution of marriage by promoting fidelity and commitment among gays in Scandinavia, as some suggest it will do here. In fact, take-up rates on gay marriage are exceedingly small. Yale law professor William Eskridge (an advocate for gay marriage) acknowledged this when he reported in 2000 that "only 2372 couples had registered after nine years of the Danish law going into effect, 674 after four years in Norway, and only 749 couples after four years in Sweden."[28] Here again, Kurtz is helpful in illuminating our understanding:

> *Danish social theorist Henning Bech and Norwegian sociologist Rune Halvorsen offer excellent accounts of the gay marriage debates in Denmark and Norway. Bech, who is perhaps Scandinavia's most prominent gay thinker, dismisses as an implausible claim the idea that gay marriage promotes monogamy. He treats this claim as something that only served a tactical purpose during the difficult political debate.*
>
> *According to Halvorsen, many of Norway's gays imposed self-censorship during the marriage debate, in order to hide their opposition to marriage itself. The goal of the gay marriage movements in Norway and Denmark, say Halvorsen and Bech, was not marriage but social approval for homosexuality. Halvorsen goes on to suggest*

that the low numbers of registered gay couples may be understood as
a collective protest against the expectations (presumably, monogamy)
embodied in marriage.[29]

The essence of the homosexual agenda and its demand for legal marriage is not about the expansion of civil rights; this is a carefully orchestrated misunderstanding of the matter. It is a public clash of privately held worldviews, the Christian versus non-Christian, the truth versus the lie. As such, it is Christianity and the church that stands in the way of this new moral order. Therefore, it is only natural that as same-sex marriage gains traction, there will follow a suppression of the Christian perspective. This suppression or persecution can already be observed in other countries. As mentioned earlier, Western nations have implemented legislative measures designed to criminalize and suppress public criticism of homosexuality. The same-sex debate in Norway was exploited by the media, resulting in the solid establishment of the liberal leadership in the state-led church.

Harvard professor of law Mary Ann Glendon acknowledged this real consequence of legitimizing same-sex marriage. She wrote,

Religious freedom, too, is at stake. As much as one may wish to live
and let live, the experience in other countries reveals that once these
arrangements become law, there will be no live-and-let-live policy
for those who differ. Gay-marriage proponents use the language of
openness, tolerance and diversity, yet one foreseeable effect of their
success will be to usher in an era of intolerance and discrimination
the likes of which we have rarely seen before. Every person and every
religion that disagrees will be labeled as bigoted and openly discrimi-
nated against. The ax must fall most heavily on religious persons and
groups that don't go along. Religious institutions will be hit with
lawsuits if they refuse to compromise their principles.[30]

Marriage is simply the highest of all human relationships and therefore must never be entered into lightly. It is the means of procreating humanity, nurturing and training subsequent generations, producing social order, and, for the Christian, the best means for perpetuating the gospel. Marriage cannot be arbitrarily redefined without undermining society's perception of and commitment to this invaluable institution and, in so doing, marriage defined as anything becomes nothing at all. This would be analogous to awarding *every* player in college football the Heisman Trophy. The Heisman Trophy, which recognizes the best collegiate football player in the country, would no longer hold its special distinction and, for that reason, would inevitably reduce in value. No one would care about receiving the Heisman because it wouldn't mean anything. In the same way, marriage redefined to accommodate a multitude of relationships also becomes meaningless.

Given the fact that marriage, as it has been traditionally understood in virtually every human society, is an important social good associated with an impressively broad array of positive benefits for society, it is imperative this institution be preserved in the strictest traditional and natural form. If marriage is allowed to die, future generations will likely inherit a godless culture. We simply must give an answer in defense of biblical marriage that persuades the culture to protect and esteem the biblical design for human relationships, family structure, and social order—for the sake of the gospel in America.

CHAPTER 8

Feminism:
Refuting Christianity as Oppressive to Women

There are those who argue that Christianity is inherently oppressive to women—that the church has institutionalized the subjugation of women to men and is largely responsible for the inequality suffered by women throughout the centuries. While there is no doubt the church has at times been complicit in the suppression of women (and in some cases continues to express these same attitudes), the fact is that such a position is not a uniquely biblical construction but rather a common social and cultural construction—one that Christianity alone has challenged.

From the beginning of human history, women have, in virtually every civilization and culture, been treated as inferior to men and forced to live as second-class citizens. A casual reflection upon history and the world today will reveal this has been and continues to be the norm throughout most of the world. Simply consider the world of Islamic fundamentalism, where women remain among the most denigrated in history. The liberation of Afghanistan, for example, revealed a culture in which women were denied virtually every freedom that we take for granted in the West. The United Nations Committee on Elimination of Discrimination Against Women (CEDAW), while conceding that conditions for women have improved in some countries, says that overall global discrimination is worsening, prompting one committee member to say,

> *Women continue to be subject to persistent discrimination in education, employment, health and nationality. Violence against women and sexual exploitation remain serious problems, despite government efforts to address the issue.*[1]

For example, every year an estimated two million young girls undergo female circumcision,[2] a horrendous and barbaric practice common in twenty-six African countries.[3] While most victims live in Africa and Asia, an increasing number can be found among immigrant and refugee families in Western Europe and North America.[4] Son preference affects women in many countries, particularly in Asia. Its consequences can be anything from female infanticide to neglect of a female child over her brother in terms of such essential needs as nutrition, basic health care, and education. In China and India, some women choose to terminate their pregnancies when expecting daughters but carry their pregnancies to term when expecting sons. In some countries, weddings are still preceded by the payment of an agreed-upon dowry by the bride's family. Failure to pay the dowry can lead to violence. In predominantly Hindu India, an average of five women a day are burned in dowry-related disputes — and many more cases are never reported. India, the second-most-populated nation in the world, only just recently criminalized spousal abuse, although its prevalence remains culturally accepted. Countries such as Pakistan, Bangladesh, and India are particularly notorious for acid attacks and so-called honor killings, in which family members murder a woman for perceived moral transgressions such as talking to a man in public or marrying without family approval.[5] Throughout the Middle East and North Africa, women are denied equal rights with men with respect to marriage, divorce, child custody, and inheritance.[6] Without a doubt, the subjugation and denigration of women is a universal evil; it is only the Christianization of cultures and, more specifically, the actions and teachings of Jesus Christ that have and continue to raise challenges to this real and devastating effect of the Fall. "The birth of Jesus," said one observer, "was the turning point for woman."[7]

DEFINING FEMINISM

When taking up the issue of feminism, it is important to note that it is not a unified, coherent movement. There are "liberal, Marxist, radical, socialist, psychoanalytic, existentialist, postmodern, neopagan and black feminism (or womanism)."[8] In other words, feminism incorporates a wide variety of worldviews and beliefs. My intent is to equip you with a response to all who presuppose that Christianity is inherently patriarchal and, therefore, oppressive to women. In point of fact, it is only the truth of Jesus Christ and the Christian view of reality that offers women, or anyone for that matter, a legitimate basis for true and sincere equality.

Leonard Swidler defined a feminist as "a person who is in favor of, and who promotes the equality of women with men, a person who advocates and practices treating women primarily as human persons (as men are so treated) and willingly contravenes social customs in so acting."[9] Using this definition, the case can be made not only that Christianity and feminism are compatible but also that any real notion of equality between the sexes is dependent upon the biblical life and worldview.

Mardi Keyes, noted Christian scholar and codirector of the L'Abri Fellowship in Massachusetts, made the point that *we must admit from the start that Christians and feminists have been guilty of stereotyping one another without reading each other's literature, or even talking to each other. Many Christians unfairly equate all "feminism" with self-centered careerism, the breakdown of the family, the wholesale rejection of men, and rebellion against God. Many non-Christian feminists equate Christianity and "the church" with the worst of "patriarchy" and male chauvinism.*[10]

Most non-Christian feminists seem unaware of the fact that following the legalization of Christianity in AD 313, the teachings of Christ so moved Emperor Valentinian I that he repealed the thousand-year-old *patria potestas*—the Roman law that conferred rights of *paterfamilias* on married men. Under *paterfamilias*, the man had supreme authority over his children even when grown, including grandchildren. He alone had the power to divorce his wife; he also possessed the power to execute his children. Under *patria potestas*, these same rights were given to men over their wives, including the right to execute their wives and the wives of their sons. *Patria potestas* and its corollary *paterfamilias* also prohibited women from speaking in public and giving testimony in court. This had been the norm throughout the civilized world for the course of a millennium. It was only due to the coming of Christ that these ideas were set aside against the revelation of God through Christ Jesus.

In order to have any meaningful dialogue on this matter with those outside the church, we must humbly concede that the Christian church hasn't always lived up to its ideals. Women have, throughout the centuries, suffered many abuses and the denial of basic human rights in the name of the Christian God. Harsh patriarchy has at times been the norm within the Christian community; the female side of creation has no doubt been made to feel as if male domination and female subjugation were ordained by God. However, when one actually examines the teachings of Jesus and the Bible, one discovers that the Christian God is actually the foremost advocate of equality between the sexes.

THE DEBATE OVER GENDERED LANGUAGE

One of the initial obstacles to meaningful dialogue with feminists is the issue of gendered language used in Scripture. This is a major issue in feminist theology, in which some theologians desire to eliminate all gendered language from Scripture. Keyes added,

> Radical feminist Mary Daly attacks the fatherhood of God saying, "If God is male, then the male is god." But I would argue that the biblical writers do not equate God's fatherhood with maleness. The intention of gendered God-language in the Bible — metaphors, images and pronouns whether male or female — is not to communicate that God is a sexual being. God is Spirit. He created and transcends sexuality. Gendered God language in the Bible communicates the personal nature of God who relates to His people as a personal being and not as an impersonal object or force.[11]

Thus, we must make clear that the Bible's use of gendered language in describing God does not communicate a preference for the male over the female. There are times when the Bible uses maternal language to describe attributes and aspects of God, such as Isaiah 49:15: "Can a mother forget the baby at her breast?" In just the same way, this passage does not indicate that God is female.

WHAT THE BIBLE SAYS ABOUT THE SEXES

So what does the Bible say about men and women? Does the Bible encourage the oppression of women as some suggest? The Bible teaches clearly that man and woman were created equal in the image of God. Genesis 1:27 states, "God created man in his own image, in the image of God he created him; male and female he created them" (ESV). As Keyes points out, the creation of humanity, male and female, in God's image "gives a powerful basis for the equal value and dignity of every human being. . . . Genesis also mandates work, the building of families and culture, care for the environment—all as shared male and female responsibilities"[12] (see Genesis 1:28; 2:15,18). The complementary contributions of each sex were needed in all areas of life and work.

It is clear from the biblical account of creation that men and women were created as equals—as complementary partners necessary for the fulfillment of the dominion mandate. In fact, when God surveyed His creation, He found that the only thing that was *not* good was the fact that Adam was alone. Some have examined this text and concluded that because God's response was the provision of a "helper," this meant that Eve was Adam's subordinate. However, the Hebrew word used is *ezer*, which literally translated means an "indispensable aid or rescuer." Keyes added, "In the twenty-one times [*ezer*] appears in the Old Testament it almost always refers to God, the mighty helper of His people."[13] This would never imply subordination. Prior to the Fall, there was perfect cooperation and fellowship between the sexes.

WHAT CHANGED?

Of course, when Adam and Eve rebelled against God's command, this all changed. Sin entered the world, and among the many ruinous effects to follow were "sexual hierarchy, rivalry and exploitation."[14] The erosion of the male/female relationship from that which God intended thus began; division, distrust, and sexism entered the world. Genesis 3 explains the tragic consequences that would follow: Her desire would be for the man, and he would rule over her. This is often misunderstood as a commandment from God, but actually God was describing what the world would be like as a result of their sin and alienation from Him. The world would no longer be as it was when all was good.

However, "as with the other results of the Fall, sickness and death, pain in childbirth, alienation from nature, and work—the appropriate human response is not resignation but resistance."[15] Men must resist their sinful desire to exploit their physical power to dominate. The picture of marriage given in Scripture describes the marital relationship as one in which husband and wife are clearly equal but assigned different roles. And each is called to *mutual* submission: "Wives, submit to your own husbands, as to the Lord" (Ephesians 5:22, ESV). This passage describes the disposition of the woman's heart and not a command to subjugate her. The admonition to men given in this same passage is even stronger: "Husbands, love your wives, as Christ loved the church and gave himself up for her, that he might sanctify her, having cleansed her by the washing of water with the word, so that he might present the church to himself in splendor, without spot or wrinkle or any such thing, that she might be holy and without blemish" (verses 25-27, ESV). Christ is certainly the head over the church, but He rules in perfect love and justice, and His defining act on behalf of the church was one of submitting to death on the cross. Christ assumed His responsibility in redeeming the church, and we are to assume our responsibilities in response to His grace. Likewise, husbands are to assume their responsibilities on *behalf* of their wives, and wives are to respond to their husbands as they would to Christ; Christ loves them, and therefore He leads them. Any attempt to subordinate women to a position of lesser importance or value than men is a perversion of this doctrine.

The Christian worldview answers the question *What has gone wrong with the world?* by revealing the history of the Fall. It is man's rebellion against God that has brought death and suffering into the world. Fellowship with God, with each other, and between men and women has been adversely affected. In light of this reality, Christians are compelled to constantly test their thoughts and motives against Scripture. When we do this, we will likely find we are certainly capable of being wrong in our attitudes and disposition toward others.

JESUS DEMONSTRATES GOD'S ATTITUDE TOWARD WOMEN

Up to this point, I have demonstrated that the biblical teaching about men and women most assuredly underscores the equal value and dignity of both men and women. Nowhere in Scripture do you find any justification for the subordination or mistreatment of women. However, the most powerful statement regarding God's egalitarian view of the sexes is demonstrated in the coming of Jesus Christ. It is through Christ that God most profoundly demonstrated *His* (and therefore what should be *our*) attitude toward women (as well as all people, for that matter).

Jesus came into a world where, in law and life, women were treated as inferior in every way. By His teaching and behavior, He continually challenged the patriarchal norms of His culture. Rejecting the practice of keeping women separate and silent, Jesus included them in His traveling band of disciples (theological students). He surprised everyone by rebuking Martha for her preoccupation with "women's work" (cooking and serving men), and praising her sister Mary for choosing to study theology with the men (see Luke 10:39-42).[16]

It is important to note that the phrase "sitting at the feet" used in reference to Mary in Luke 10:39 is the same technical phrase used by the apostle Paul to describe his rabbinic training "at the feet of Gamaliel" in Acts 22:3 (NKJV).

A common facet of Near Eastern culture was to blame women for male lust, but Jesus completely subverted this when He charged that it was men who looked lustfully at women who were at fault in the sight of God (see Matthew 5:28). To the Romans, a woman's perspective was so worthless that she wasn't permitted to testify in court, yet Jesus, who was fully God, chose women to be the first witnesses of His resurrection. Everything about Jesus and His followers challenged the patriarchal norms of the day.

Writing as only a woman could, Dorothy Sayers, the renowned British author and close friend of C. S. Lewis, said this about Jesus:

Perhaps it is no wonder that the women were first at the cradle and last at the cross. They had never known a man like this Man—there never has been such another. A prophet and teacher who never nagged at them, never flattered or coaxed or patronized; who never made jokes about them, never treated them either as "The women, God help us!" or "The ladies, God bless them!"; who rebuked without querulousness and praised without condescension; who took their questions and arguments seriously; who never mapped out their sphere for them, never urged them to be feminine or jeered at them for being female; who had no axe to grind and no uneasy male dignity to defend; who took them as he found them and was completely unselfconscious. There is no act, no sermon, no parable in the whole Gospel that borrows its pungency from female perversity; nobody could possibly guess from the words and deeds of Jesus that there was anything "funny" about woman's nature.[17]

How can we not be moved by this Jesus, and how can we not share this truth with those who err in their condemnation of Christianity? No doubt there have been many throughout the ages who have failed—and we continue to fail—to live up to these standards. However, the Christian faith should not be judged solely by the actions of some Christians who have suffered the influence of their time and culture, in spite of their convictions. I, too, would confess that the very examination of this subject in preparation for this book revealed the presence of certain culturally induced perspectives that I had to lay at the cross. In the end, Christianity rests on the person and work of Jesus Christ; on this point, no other figure in history has served to advance the equal value and dignity of women more than Jesus!

JESUS RELATIVIZED ALL RACE, CLASS, AND SEX DISTINCTIONS

Consider the changes in religious practice that followed the coming of Christ—changes that would radically challenge a patriarchal Jewish society. Whereas the sign of membership in the community of God's people was previously circumcision, following Pentecost it became baptism. The radical inclusiveness of this change is expressed in Paul's letter to the Galatians: "All of you who were baptized into Christ have clothed yourself with Christ. There is neither Jew nor Greek, slave nor free, male nor female, for you are all one in Christ Jesus" (3:27-28). This passage reveals the character and intent of God's inbreaking reign, in which all racial, class, age, and gender distinctions are relativized in Christ! For the early Christians, these were not simply religious platitudes or ideals but an actual way of living. In fact, "the inclusiveness and love evident in the early Christian church . . . were so real and dramatic, that some in the Roman world called the Christians 'the third race.'"[18] With the coming of Christ, marriage changed dramatically from one-sided male rule to mutual submission—the wife submitting to a husband who was to model Christ by loving her enough to die for her, "that she might be holy and without blemish" (see Ephesians 5:21-33, ESV). Paul described marriage as mutual authority, in which husbands and wives have exactly the same authority over their own and each other's bodies (see 1 Corinthians 7:4). Keyes makes the point, "This is far from the 'satellite' marriage model, with wife revolving around her husband and his needs."[19]

RADICAL FEMINISM FAILS

Thus far we have examined feminism from the simple perspective of equality—a concept that not only is compatible with Christianity but actually emanates from biblical teaching and finds its ultimate authority in the person of Christ. By contrast, the more radicalized versions of feminism that have stirred the public consciousness transcend mere equality and argue that there are ontological or innate moral differences between men and women. Men are seen as inherently evil oppressors and women are inherently innocent and, as such, subject to victimization. Consider the following statements by some of the more prominent radical feminists. Susan Brownmiller wrote that all men are essentially rapists,[20] Marilyn French wrote that "all men hate all women,"[21] and Andrea Dworkin wrote that marital intercourse was merely another form of male domination, or "occupation" in a military sense.[22] Women, these writers argued, are intrinsically good, sympathetic, cooperative, caring, nurturing, and peace loving.[23] In other words, women, unlike men, do not possess an inherent sin nature. Of course, statements like these are simply preposterous. If they were true, then there wouldn't be any women's prisons—and yet there are. As the father of two daughters, a brother to three sisters, and a husband to one (nearly perfect, so she tells me) wife, one thing I am certain of is that sin is a universal human condition affecting both men and women.

While there is no doubt that many women have suffered as a result of male oppression, abuse, and violence, it would be a grave mistake to regard this conduct as merely the product of male character and not the universal condition of sin. It is sin that renders all men *and* women equidistant from God, and it is this condition that only Christ can remedy. Radical feminism obscures this fact by suggesting it isn't sin that is the source of humanity's problem but maleness and patriarchy. The tragic fact is that both men and women struggle with the same kinds of things that can undermine any human relationship and community—"pride, dominance, greed, self-centeredness and even violence. . . . No sex, race or class is free from the sin that ruins relationships, exploits power, or starts wars."[24] It is precisely as Aleksandr Solzhenitsyn, writing about the Soviet forced labor camps in *The Gulag Archipelago*, said, "The line separating good and evil passes . . . through every human heart."[25]

THE BIBLICAL DOCTRINE OF SIN OFFERS HOPE

Many today perceive the biblical doctrine of sin to be a pessimistic barrier to human progress. However, where sin is our shared problem, the opportunity for change exists. By understanding sin as a universal condition with which I am infected, I can both repent and forgive. When I have sinned, I can apologize; I can ask for forgiveness. And when I am wronged, I can offer grace, knowing I am in need of the same. By accepting the universal condition of sin, reconciliation is possible. There is no room for self-righteousness when we understand that our problem is one shared by all human beings. Using race, gender, and other distinctions to condemn, criticize, and classify people are simply symptoms of this deeper sin problem in which our natural inclination is to love ourselves more than others. Even painful relationships between men and women and between different racial and ethnic groups can know real healing, although not to perfection because no relationships can be perfect in this broken world. As L'Abri founder Edith Schaeffer reportedly said, "The Utopian who demands perfection or nothing will always get the nothing and will do a lot of damage in the process."[26]

So when speaking to the radical feminist or simply that person who has bought into the popular conception that Christianity is inherently oppressive to women, what would you say? Without the God of the Bible, who has revealed Himself in Scripture and in the person of Christ, you can't argue with the attitudes reflected by the nineteenth-century playwright and novelist Honoré de Balzac, who wrote,

Pay no attention to [woman's] murmurs, her cries, her pains; nature has made her for our use and for bearing everything: children, sorrows, blows and pains inflicted by man. Do not accuse yourself of hardness. In all the codes of so-called civilized nations, man has written the laws that ranged woman's destiny under this bloody epigraph: "Vae victus! Woe to the weak!"[27]

If impersonal and amoral nature is the final reality, how can one legitimately argue with Balzac? There is no logical reason whatsoever why the stronger should *not* dominate the weaker. This is, according to the Darwinian worldview, necessary for the survival and propagation of the species, is it not? Why shouldn't men assert control over women if they can? In the absence of God, what moral authority would compel them not to? Attempts to deny or legislate against this tendency to dominate would be arbitrary and thus hold no real authority for the preservation of this or that moral position. Conversely, any position that advocates for the domination of women is also arbitrary and, logically speaking, must be equally valid. In an impersonal universe, there is no overarching authority upon which these moral positions rest and final justice depends. The atheist might argue on the basis of sociability and mutual cooperation that men should treat women as equals. However, men have, throughout history, treated women as inferior subjects, yet their societies, including Christian societies, have not only endured but also prospered. So sociability and mutual cooperation are *not* adequate to promote the inherent value of women. There is but one basis for the equal dignity and treatment of women: the God and Creator as revealed to us in holy Scripture! The abandonment of this basis will not liberate women but, in fact, will surrender the only hope women actually have, as one Christian feminist so aptly warned:

As Western culture has discarded belief in the Judeo-Christian God, we have lost the most powerful philosophical-religious base for the feminist belief in the equal value, dignity and rights of all persons, including women. Secularism cannot produce an equivalent foundation. The biblical worldview provides a powerful moral authority for denouncing sexism, racism and all injustice as wrong. Rape, incest and violence against women are always and absolutely wrong—not because feminists say so but because these things violate God's character and laws. . . . Human outrage at injustice is not a freakish quirk in an impersonal and amoral universe. Our sense of justice corresponds with God's, because we are made in His image. And there is the promise that one day, all will be made right by a just and merciful Creator. Without such a hope, injustice is bound to have the final word.[28]

Is Christianity *inherently* oppressive to women, or is it instead God's gracious intervention on their behalf? No other culture, outside of those transformed by Christianity, has even raised the issue of equality between the sexes; as noted at the beginning of the chapter, many cultures still do not afford basic human rights to women. Ironically, the only criticisms of patriarchy and appeals for the equal treatment of women appear within Christianized societies. This is a natural result of the uniquely Christian conception that because human beings are made in the image of God, they have equal value and dignity—a concept that stands in stark contrast to the fallen world where oppression, malice, and envy sadly remain the norm.

CHAPTER 9

New Age Spirituality: Filling the Spiritual Vacuum

As we conclude our examination of those forces that present obstacles to the reception of the gospel, we simply must address what has been called New Age spirituality. While this term may conjure up images of crystals, incense, and Shirley MacLaine for many of us, the fact is the church, either by abandonment of its cultural responsibilities or its capitulation to the culture, has created a spiritual vacuum that the New Age religious movement is now pressing to fill.

While so-called New Age spirituality has been a fringe element for the last forty to fifty years, I believe that with the convergence of postmodern thought (which, again, posits that life is without point, purpose, or meaning), New Age spirituality has become an attractive—or at least the latest—alternative to this untenable position. I say untenable because the idea of life being meaningless defies the very nature of who we are as human beings, made in the image of God. Man cannot remain satisfied in such a state; therefore, he is innately compelled to render his life meaningful and with some purpose.

Granted, meaningful efforts are not likely to receive much support in a hedonistic culture such as ours. This makes men and women all the more vulnerable to the inane and often nebulous answers offered up by the world of New Age thought.

EASTERN MYSTICISM IN WESTERN DRESS

But what exactly *is* New Age spirituality? In essence, New Age spirituality is anything but new; in fact, it is nothing more than the revival of ancient pagan religious thought that is monistic or pantheistic in nature. Pantheism in this sense is the belief that "god" is either related to or integrated into the forces in the universe—in other words, an impersonal force that one can learn to tap into or manipulate for personal benefit (that is, the *Star Wars* concept of religion). Monism is slightly different in that it holds to the belief that "everything is one, that reality is one unitary organic whole with no independent parts."[1] In other words, you and I are not distinct from anything or anyone else; instead, we are part of the larger essence or whole.

New Age spirituality is nothing more than Eastern mysticism in "Western dress."[2] In his book *True Truth*, Art Lindsley compared New Age religion to beef stew:

> *Everybody knows what beef stew is like. But just because you have had one beef stew, it does not mean you have had them all. Cooks put in different cuts of beef, different vegetables and different spices. Likewise New Age spirituality draws from various Eastern religious traditions, such as Hinduism, Buddhism and Taoism, and it may include Native American and shamanistic practices.[3]*

And, I might add, many in the West are now integrating elements of New Age into Christianity. Although there may be varied manifestations of New Age, Lindsley identified four principles held in common:

1. All is one.
2. You are God.
3. Altered consciousness is the goal.
4. Unlimited power is available.[4]

The key to New Age is that you, through instruction either from spiritual masters or even spiritual entities, must achieve enlightenment (understanding that all is one). In so doing, you will rise above the human condition by means of an altered consciousness and see that distinction itself is an illusion; if all is one and God is part of the all, then you are in effect God! It is this so-called enlightenment, or understanding, that will then allow you to become part of the divine and thus gain access to unlimited power.

THE EVOLUTION OF RELIGION

At odds in this new religious conflict is the proposal of a new spiritual view over and against Christianity specifically but also every other theistic religious system. This new spiritual view is presented as a natural progression in the evolution of humanity, which is merely evolving beyond the old spiritual understanding, which was inhibited by revealed religion. Ernst Haeckel (1834–1919), professor of zoology at the University of Jena (Thuringia, Germany), was one of the leading scientific voices in Europe in the latter nineteenth century and a prominent advocate of Darwinism. Haeckel wrote that in light of "our godlike reason and its clear superiority to revelation . . . we must at once dispose of this dangerous error of thinking that revelation ought to rule reason."[5] According to Haeckel, the soul—a name for our capacity to think, feel, and move—is not distinct from our biological being but is, in fact, merely a part of our biological DNA; thus, it can be understood scientifically. This has become the predominant view today when discussing the spiritual nature of man. Spiritual evolution, these scientific spiritualists suggest, is leading us into a more enlightened spiritual state that is ultimately found within oneself and *not* in the authority and revelation of a living, personal God.

Again, you can see the appeal of this idea to the modernistic mind, which holds to the progressive assumption common to the Age of Enlightenment. That being the case, the modernist is likely to embrace what he perceives to be the latest understanding of our spiritual natures. This, of course, is rooted in the Enlightenment idea that man invented God, not vice versa. The idea of a living and personal God who has revealed Himself through Scripture, history, and nature becomes more and more implausible to a modernistic mind—one that is suspect of the past, trusts in science, and is skeptical of such supernatural intervention. New Age spirituality offers many Americans, who are steeped in modernistic assumptions, a plausible basis for discarding revealed religion and the one true God.

This is why I believe that modernity, modernism, and postmodernism are so significant in creating conditions favorable to the acceptance of New Age thought. Modernity and modernism produced the necessary mindset for shifting our thoughts away from the living, personal, and supernatural God. Postmodernism provided the philosophical despair that is now driving men and women back toward a search for spiritual significance and meaning—but within the confines of a modernistic framework, a framework well suited to the spirituality espoused by New Age.

James Herrick, professor of communication at Hope College, pointed out in his book *The Making of the New Spirituality* that New Age spirituality has become so influential that it is replacing the Christian worldview as "the religious framework for a large and growing number of people in the West."[6] This syncretistic view of spirituality blends various religious beliefs—including, in some cases, Christianity—into one powerfully persuasive brand of religion that holds tremendous appeal to sinful man. For one, concepts such as sin are seen as part of the old religious order and are to be discarded, as these are obstacles to world-wide spiritual enlightenment and universal harmony. Thus, the New Age religious follower has a particular disdain for Christian theism.

EVERYTHING OLD IS NEW AGAIN!

However, as stated earlier, New Age thought is anything but new. Herrick pointed out,

> *This contemporary form of pantheistic teaching began to appear and/ or reappear in Western religious writing around 1700. Over the past three centuries, and under the guidance of numerous public advocates working in a number of genres and media, this new spiritual thought has become well entrenched in Western religious consciousness.*[7]

According to the American Religious Identity Survey conducted in 2001, the number of self-described adherents to New Age thought has increased 340 percent since 1990.[8] A decade ago, sociologists at University of California–Santa Barbara estimated that as many as 12 million Americans could be considered active participants in alternative spiritual systems and another 30 million are actively interested.[9] James Herrick added, "Perhaps 1000 to 2000 new religious movements have arisen in the U.S. alone in the twentieth century, and few of these are rooted in traditional Judeo-Christian theological assumptions."[10]

THE "OPRAHFICATION" OF EASTERN MYSTICISM

Because of the varied and numerous manifestations of this emerging spirituality, it is difficult to fully grasp its scope and influence on American culture. However, recall that Nancy Reagan sought advice from an astrologer while in the White House and Hillary Clinton solicited contact with the deceased Eleanor Roosevelt. Consider the immense popularity of Oprah Winfrey, who continually features New Age authors and advocates on her popular program.

Just last year Oprah launched a first-of-its-kind, ten-week webinar based on the book *A New Earth: Awakening to Your Life's Purpose*, by best-selling author Eckhart Tolle. This free course, led personally by both Oprah and Tolle, drew more than 750,000 registrants. Tolle, who is described as "a contemporary spiritual teacher who is not aligned with any particular religion or tradition, . . . conveys a simple yet profound message with the timeless and uncomplicated clarity of the ancient spiritual masters: There is a way out of suffering and into peace."[11] In describing the thesis of his latest book, Tolle wrote, "An essential aspect of this awakening consists in transcending our ego-based state of consciousness. This is a prerequisite not only for personal happiness but also for the ending of violent conflict endemic on our planet."[12] In other words, it is the alteration of our consciousness that is key to the salvation of men, not Jesus Christ; our shared problem is incorrect perceptions, not sin.

Tolle, who experienced "a profound inner transformation" that "radically changed the course of his life at the age of twenty-nine,"[13] became an active participant in *A Course in Miracles* in the years following. Published in 1975, *A Course in Miracles* is a spiritual self-study course primarily representing the thought system of monism, which, again, is the idea that all is one. Consider these excerpts from *A Course in Miracles*, which Oprah began offering on her website in January 2008, for free, just prior to the Tolle event:

Extend your perception beyond what your senses register (Lesson 1). That body does not mean anything. . . . One thing is like another (Lesson 1).

 Everything you see is the result of your thoughts. There is no exception to this fact. . . . Salvation requires that you also recognize that every thought you have brings either peace or war; either love or fear. To trust in the force that moves the universe is faith. Faith isn't blind, it's visionary. Faith is believing that the universe is on our side and that the universe knows what it's doing (Lesson 16).[14]

Now compare these statements to the words of the Buddha:

This whole world of delusion is nothing but a shadow caused by the mind. . . . There is no world . . . outside the mind. . . . To Buddha every definitive thing is illusion. . . . Things have no reality in themselves but are like heat haze.[15]

Buddhism, in particular, teaches that no supreme and personal God exists and that the universe is animated by an impersonal life force, which connects all things. It also teaches that one can, through spiritual enlightenment, rise above the illusion of reality and enter nirvana, a condition in which one is absorbed into the greater essence, or whole.

These are the very same principles put forth in both *A Course in Miracles* and Tolle's book *A New Earth*. The most troubling aspect is that *A Course in Miracles* employs many references to God, the Holy Spirit, and even the Son of God. In addition, there are statements such as "Surrender all outcomes to God" and "Allow the Holy Spirit to do what He does best." Of course, the instruction goes on to emphasize "the power of your own thinking," which supposedly empowers *you* to create the outcome that "serve[s] your own best interests" in *your* hands, which, according to the course, is "your only goal in any situation." The "god" presented here is a monistic, impersonal god who "is everywhere and is *in* everything," including inanimate objects. According to the course, "God is not outside of you but rather in your mind."[16] The blending of Christian terminology with New Age paganism endorsed by Oprah has already deceived many professing Christians.

I can appreciate the success of Oprah Winfrey; she seems like a kind and sincere woman. Her achievements are, indeed, impressive, given what she has overcome, and I believe she truly wants to help people and make the world a better place. However, these materials are nothing but spiritualized self-help and repackaged paganism typical of New Age spirituality, and they only serve to deceive and divert people from the One True God and the salvation that comes only through Jesus Christ.

Another of Oprah's frequent guests is Harvard graduate and former Green Beret Gary Zukav.[17] Zukav also argues that traditional religious thought, such as Christianity, serves as a barrier to this New Age evolution. It is this aspect, in particular, that makes this new spiritual view a direct threat to the gospel because its adherents know that it cannot successfully coexist with the revealed Word of the Christian faith.

MERGING SCIENCE AND SPIRITUALITY

What distinguishes Zukav is the fact that he is not some extreme occultist or self-proclaimed guru but rather a highly educated author who argues that science is key to human spiritual awareness and development. In his book *The Dancing Wu Li Masters* (winner of an American Book Club award in 1979), Zukav explored the connection between quantum physics and spirituality. In his best-selling book *The Seat of the Soul*, he wrote that the "discoveries of science illuminate both the inner and outer experiences."[18] According to Zukav, James Herrick tells us, "Science has even suggested a new understanding of God, not as the personal deity of the Judeo-Christian tradition, but as a 'conscious light,' and 'Divine intelligence' that animate not a single entity, but the universe itself."[19]

For the first time in history, we are witnessing the merging of modern science and paganism into a new and plausible religious system, one that appears devoid of the silly and primitive associations typical of ancient paganism. Despite the fact these same superstitious and facile explanations of human spirituality, rooted in ancient paganism, still remain, under the guise of New Age they are far more appealing to modern man. Zukav is but one example of a growing number of writers and celebrities who have helped popularize and elevate New Age thought into the mainstream consciousness.

Evidence for the growth of this new spirituality can be seen in the "widespread belief in angels and reincarnation; the appeal of religious and quasi-religious shrines, retreat centers, and theme parks; interest in metaphysical and theosophical teachings; prosperity theology and 'possibility thinking'; and large proportions of Americans reporting mystical experiences."[20] Consider the popularity of John Edward, the self-proclaimed psychic medium, host of *Crossing Over* and more recently *Cross Country* television programs. (Edward is another frequent guest of Oprah Winfrey.) Edward claims to have helped thousands with his uncanny ability to predict future events and communicate with those who have crossed over to the other side.[21]

RESURRECTING GNOSTICISM THROUGH FICTION

Ponder the spectacular success of Dan Brown's best-selling novel *The Da Vinci Code*. Despite the fictional genre, Brown opened his best-selling novel with this statement:

Fact: The Priory of Sion — a European secret society founded in 1099 — is a real organization. In 1975, Paris's Bibliothèque Nationale discovered parchments known as Les Dossiers Secrets, identifying numerous members of the Priory of Sion, including Sir Isaac Newton, Botticelli, Victor Hugo, and Leonardo da Vinci.

The Vatican prelature known as Opus Dei is a deeply devout Catholic group that has been the topic of recent controversy due to reports of brainwashing, coercion, and a practice known as "corporal mortification." Opus Dei has just completed construction of a $47 *million National Headquarters at 243 Lexington Avenue in New York City.*

All descriptions of artwork, architecture, documents, and secret rituals in this novel are accurate.[22]

In numerous interviews, Brown has made it quite clear that his novel is based on allegedly true — but suppressed — historical facts. In his own words,

I am not the first person to tell the story of Mary Magdalene and the Holy Grail. This idea is centuries old. I am one in a long line of people who has offered up this alternative history. The Da Vinci Code describes history as I have come to understand it through many years of travel, research, reading, interviews, and exploration.[23]

Brown's novel has contributed significantly to a renewed interest in — and given new authority to — the long-ago-debunked Gnostic gospels. The Gnostic gospels are a dubious class of writings about the life of Jesus that are associated with the third-century mystical trend of Gnostic Christianity; they contradict the New Testament description of Jesus. Although estimated to have originated in the latter half of the third century, the earliest actual manuscripts are from the fourteenth century. Gnostic teaching was addressed and declared heresy by the early church, given their lack of apostolic authority and fraudulent authorship.

FENG SHUI AND OTHER SILLY NOTIONS

Consider the growing popularity of feng shui in contemporary Western architectural and interior design. Feng shui (pronounced "fung shway") is the ancient Chinese practice of placement and arrangement of space to achieve harmony with the environment. The literal translation is "wind and water." One feng shui practitioner boasted, "You can have everything you desire, you just have to know how to make it happen. The simple and easy secrets to having all the abundance, the wealth and the riches are here for the asking."[24] The secret being offered here is reducible to the proper placement of one's furniture relative to the building and its occupants. In other words, the reason you may be suffering from poor health, financial disappointment, and life dissatisfaction is because your La-Z-Boy is facing the wrong way! You may think this an obscure belief, but consider that in April of 2006, Motorola filed a patent for a cell phone capable of "evaluating locations according to Feng Shui principles."[25] Using a combination of GPS receiver, digital camera, and other features, the phone will apparently be able to work out how harmonious your home is according to the principles of feng shui. While working in the commercial design and construction industry in the 1980s, I myself began to encounter feng shui consultants on major commercial projects in the United States.

The plethora of literature espousing goddess worship, Gnosticism, and other New Age concepts has exploded in the last decade. In fact, according to a report in the *Los Angeles Times*, "sales of religious books skyrocketed 150% from 1991 to 1997, compared to 35% for the rest of the industry"[26] — and the majority of these books are not those of the historical Christian perspective. James Herrick added that "these figures do not reflect the enormous sales of books on spiritual themes that are ostensibly devoted to business success, medicine and healing, relationships and science."[27]

There are a host of additional expressions of New Age that we simply do not have time to address. However, let me offer a brief survey of some: Wicca, the neo-pagan practice of witchcraft and nature worship, claims more than 1.4 million members in the United States. There is goddess worship, shamanism, UFO encounters and alien world theories (L. Ron Hubbard's Scientology), Druidism and the worship of ancient Norse gods, and Native American religions. Even within so-called Christian circles, you have the prosperity doctrine of the Word-Faith movement, which treats faith as a tangible force that you can learn to tap into for personal benefit. In other words, it is *your* faith, and the strength of your faith compels God to bless you—or in the case of weak faith, hinders Him from blessing you. There are the medieval mystical Jewish teachings of Kabbalah, a practice being made popular again by Madonna, Demi Moore, and other Hollywood celebrities. This is simply one of the latest examples of the attraction Gnosticism has for many Americans. In his book *The American Religion*, Yale professor Harold Bloom argued that many Americans, even some professing Christians, are Gnostics of sorts. Their religion is based on personal experience and has little room for tradition or authority. The goal of their religion, he writes, is "to be alone with God or Jesus"[28]—again, a notion well-suited to the radical individualism prevalent within the post-Enlightenment West.

Additionally, there is Buddhism, which has increased in number of adherents by more than 269 percent in America since 1990.[29] The Dalai Lama's book *Ethics for the New Millennium* is one of the most popular business books ever written, remaining atop the best-seller's list for more than nine weeks in 2001, selling more copies than Stephen Covey or Bill Gates. (The Dalai Lama is another frequent guest of Oprah Winfrey.) It is ironic that the leading Tibetan Buddhist would write on the subject of business ethics, given the fact that Buddhism, logically followed, encourages social apathy. If reality is an illusion and the ultimate goal is individual/private enlightenment, what contribution can Buddhism make to solving the world's real problems? Professor of religion Robert E. Hume was correct when he wrote in *The World's Living Religions* that, in one sense, "the main trend in Buddhist ethics is negative, repressive, quietistic, non-social,"[30] a fact admitted by Buddhists who nonetheless argue that the self-satisfaction offered by Buddhism is reason enough to become a Buddhist. So the idea that (1) there are actual ethical distinctions, some of which are presumably good; and (2) these distinctions should then be pressed into what Buddhists believe is an illusory reality, is in complete contradiction to the very teachings of Buddhism.

CARL JUNG AND THE SOPHISTICATION OF NEW AGE

Then there is the late Carl Jung (1875–1961). A founder of modern psychoanalysis, Jung is more influential in counseling circles today than Freud. Due in part to his scholarly appeal, which helped create a more sophisticated interpretation of primitive mystical spirituality, few people have had more influence than Jung in advancing the New Age spirituality. By presenting his ideas within a pseudo-scientific framework, Jung was able to retrieve for "modern Westerners many ancient Eastern, Gnostic, and cultic ideas, such as the divinity of the individual, the existence of spiritual *gnosis*, the reality of a spiritual elite, and the legitimacy of parapsychological phenomenon."[31] A leading expert on Jung's spiritual ideas, Richard Noll wrote that "such ancient ideas, ironically, are what Jung is best known for introducing as modern innovations."[32] Noll commented that these ideas are "so widely spread in our culture through their connections to psychotherapeutic practice, New Age spirituality and neopaganism that they continue to be the subject of innumerable workshops, TV shows, bestselling books, and videos that they form the basis of a brand of psychotherapy with its own trade name: Jungian Analysis."[33]

Jungian analyst Edward Edinger acknowledges Jung was a twentieth-century prophet, "a voice ushering in a new religious age."[34] Edinger refered to Jung's *Collected Works* as "a divinely inspired 'new dispensation' to succeed the Jewish and Christian dispensations of the Old and New Testaments."[35] James Herrick pointed out that "Jung's works are read as part of the services of a New Age 'Gnostic Church' in San Francisco, as they are alongside the works of Emerson at some Unitarian services."[36] Jung himself held that "all religious traditions would be transcended by a religious consciousness much richer and more encompassing than any that had yet been manifested."[37]

One of the more disturbing aspects of Carl Jung was his early interest in the Volkish movement, which swept through central Europe in the 1890s. The Volkish movement was a utopian mystical belief that rejected Christianity and emphasized the worship of nature, in particular the sun. The popularity of the Volkish movement, with its foundational concept of an Aryan elite, actually may have contributed to the preconditions necessary for the rise of Nazism in Germany.[38] One scholar wrote, "By 1933 the German right was captured by Volkish ideas. It was a trend in German thought that became so strong that millions accepted it as the only solution to Germany's problems."[39] Jung was regarded as an important proponent of Volkish thinking, a connection that many followers of Jung have worked very hard to conceal, for obvious reasons.

HOW NEW AGE SPIRITUALITY UNDERMINES THE GOSPEL

So how are the basic tenets of New Age spirituality actually shifting Western religious thought away from Christianity? Here again, James Herrick is helpful in defining seven foundational concepts common to New Age thinking, which find support from the cultural influences discussed in the first section.

1. *History is not spiritually important.*

History as a record of events in space and time has no particular significance to the spiritual understanding or progress of the individual human being or of religious communities. In fact, history as traditionally understood may be a hindrance to spirituality by tying people to local beliefs, particular places and individual teachers. Records that purport to be spiritual histories, such as the Bible, are not historical as much as they are symbolic, allegorical and mythical.[40]

You can see how postmodernism in particular has proven helpful in preparing the Western mind to accept this notion. Under postmodern influence, history is written by those in power and therefore bears their bias—thus, it cannot be trusted. This idea was popularized in *The Da Vinci Code*, about which the author wrote,

Since the beginning of recorded time, history has been written by the "winners" (those societies and belief systems that conquered and survived). . . . Many historians now believe (as do I) that in gauging the historical accuracy of a given concept, we should first ask ourselves a far deeper question: How historically accurate is history itself?[41]

2. *The dominance of reason.*

Reason . . . is the divine characteristic in humans. Reason is virtually unlimited in its potential for development through scientific study, mystical experience, and evolution. Reason is the principal means for human apprehension of spiritual truth, with the most substantial spiritual insights coming to those with the greatest awareness.[42]

While the New Age thinker is convinced he is exercising reason, he is, in essence, more emotive—in search of personal experience, not verifiable fact. He is able to validate this position as being reasonable by dismissing knowable facts in the traditional sense (particularly historical facts), as being illusory and not representing spiritual reality (thus the need for the first tenet). This is very helpful when trying to defend New Age thought. One can simply argue (irrationally) that those of us who do not comprehend these new spiritual truths are bound by traditional or outdated modes of thinking.

3. *The spiritualization of science.*

Science, the empirical study of the material universe, is the primary instrument reason employs to acquire spiritual knowledge. Science is both the source and test of theology—it discovers new spiritual truths and confirms what has long been known to human beings through certain spiritual traditions.[43]

This is observed almost daily as one scientist after another offers theories that purport to explain our spiritual natures in terms limited to biological causes and not supernatural possibilities that defy human explanation. However, as we have seen with Kinsey, Freud, and Jung, science is often used and manipulated to serve the scientist's own biases and presuppositions about reality. Science, which has historically concerned itself with materialistic causes, now seeks to integrate God into the material universe. Here again, modernity conditions us to accept any truth claimed in the name of science.

4. *The animation of nature.*

Nature is infused with a divine spirit, consciousness, or life force (Monism). Physical nature is thus alive with divine energy or soul. In short, nature is divine. This fact about physical nature warrants its study by science as a source of spiritual knowledge.[44]

This is most apparent among the radical environmentalist movement and the growing elevation of animals to a status equal to humans, prompting new terms such as *speciesism*, in which the biblical hierarchy whereby animals are subservient to man is deemed immoral.

5. *Hidden knowledge and spiritual progress.*

Knowledge of the spiritual world is seen as key to spiritual prog-
ress. Such knowledge allegedly comes by means of reason employing
science, but it may also come through certain individuals specially
gifted to understand and directly experience the spiritual realm.
Spiritual knowledge, then, is the special preserve of extraordinarily
gifted individuals including some scientists, but also a new class
of shamans, mediums between the physical and spiritual realms.
Because this knowledge is not immediately accessible to all people, it
is, at least initially, hidden or secret.[45]

The combination of the cult of scientific experts with our consumerist habits makes for an ideal culture into which one can market
one's "special knowledge" to people searching for meaning and significance—in the same way they shop for clothes!

6. *Spiritual evolution.*

Human beings are destined to realize unimaginable spiritual advance-
ment through a process of spiritual evolution. Spiritual evolution is
not simply change, but advancement that occurs incrementally over
time. The eventual result of this process of spiritual evolution will be
actual human divinity. Through science, the means of directing and
hastening this process is within our grasp.[46]

Here again, one sees how the contribution of modernism makes
this idea plausible. The progressive assumption inherent in modernistic thinking gives credibility to this assertion. This idea satisfies the
desire of the modernist looking for meaning and purpose but within
an acceptable mental framework. There is nothing here that challenges
his present presuppositions in regard to reality. There is only new and

improved information that one can easily integrate into his current worldview.

   7. *Religious pluralism as rooted in mystical experience.*

The only universal religious experience is the mystical experience. Thus, mysticism provides a basis for religious pluralism, for the uniting of disparate spiritual traditions around common mystical insights. There is a steadily increasing awareness of this fact within each religious tradition.[47]

This idea appeals to and is supported by the "all paths lead to god" postmodern crowd. As stated in chapter 3, postmodernism destroys the healthy pluralism that allows for different ideas, views, and perspectives; ultimately, it even destroys such concepts as conversion. Where a healthy plurality of ideas exists, there remains the notion that some of these ideas may, in fact, be false and thus conversion to the truth remains possible. The pluralism promoted within the New Age movement is very postmodern in the sense that there is no longer the possibility that any particular understanding of spirituality may be false—unless, of course, it claims to be the exclusive truth.

TESTING THEIR CLAIMS

But are these perspectives true? Is there any rational basis upon which one can objectively examine and accept or reject these teachings or religious interpretations of reality? Unlike New Age mysticism, which rests on myth, secret knowledge, or the purely subjective claims derived from the private mystical experiences of certain individuals, Christianity is grounded in history. John Stott, a contemporary theologian and scholar, pointed out, "Christianity does not only rest on a historical person, Jesus of Nazareth, but on certain historical events which involved Him, especially his birth, death, and resurrection."[48] So history provides an objective foundation from which one can examine and verify the spiritual claims and events associated with Jesus and, in so doing, limit theological speculation to objective facts. New Age religious claims have no such foundation. Instead, one is asked to trust the self-proclaimed mediums, gurus, and (in some cases) scientists that their personal interpretation of life's most important questions is, in fact, true—apart from any objective or verifiable basis whatsoever. One is simply asked to blindly trust in the individual mythical interpretations of persons completely unknown to them—interpretations of what are, essentially, nothing more than the repackaging of primitive religions that once sought to explain natural phenomena, such as the rising of the sun.

In Christianity, history has been the scene of God's acts of intervention and, ultimately, of redemption. The Bible presents a historical account of God's interaction with humanity, offers insight into spiritual reality, and gives meaning to history. In so doing, we are given an explanation of reality that on some level is testable. We know, for example, that man does not have to be *taught* how to sin. As our experience with reality demonstrates, this comes naturally, and Scripture explains, in the only way plausible, why this is so. We know, for example, that the biblical story includes the prediction of certain events that also have real spiritual significance. And we know that these events came to pass just as predicted. The Bible gives humanity some understanding about the world and ourselves that we could not otherwise know unless given by the One who created all things. This knowledge is not abstract mysticism but verifiable knowledge that coincides with reality and human experience. On this point Christianity stands alone, providing an objective, external foundation for human spiritual experience and religious teaching.

CONFUSING REASON WITH THE AUTONOMOUS SELF

As for reason being the instrument of spiritual enlightenment, the Bible warns us of the reliance upon reason. While it is true that God, making us in His image, gave us the ability to reason (and certainly God expects us to exercise reason in the understanding of our faith), our ability to understand God (and those things that have not been *revealed* to humanity) remains beyond our intellectual capacities. Thus, Christian reason originates in and emanates from God's revelation to humanity. In other words, human reason has its limits, as the writer of Proverbs states: "Trust in the LORD with all your heart and lean not on your own understanding" (Proverbs 3:5). The mind and rational thought are certainly to be valued, but nowhere in Scripture does God tell us that they alone are adequate to fathom the depths of the human soul, let alone the complete nature of God.

New Age mysticism confuses reason with the radically autonomous self. This is nothing more than spiritual narcissism, which shifts its worship from the Creator God to ourselves by claiming that the divine is within each of us, merely awaiting discovery. The problem that the New Age religious have with the ascent of reason is that, according to them, not all of us are capable of this ascent. Therefore, a spiritual or intellectual elite is created. This is best exemplified in Ayn Rand's theory of radical self-interest or Voltaire's concept that the masses of religious devotees were ignorant of spiritual truth. Logically speaking, this elitist perspective seems only natural to one who believes he is divine and thus worships himself.

In such a system one has to ask, "What moral imperatives would compel a person with such radical self-interest to exercise care and concern for his fellow man?" What possible basis would there be or could there be for morality and ethics at all? No, the reliance upon reason in this sense is not a mind operating under the authority and direction of God, to His glory, but rather an attempt to interpret the universe and everything in it, either from within ourselves or outside and apart from God. This elitism is simply unavoidable in an evolutionary framework such as that put forth by New Age religion.

As for the spiritualization of science, the twentieth century has seen the migration of science from the material world to the spiritual world. With the marginalization of Christian thought, Western science is now attempting to explore and explain those categories once considered the domain of the philosopher and theologian. Here again, James Herrick offers insight: "Thomas Paine argued that science supported, not the theistic religion of the Revealed Word, but the pantheistic religion of nature and reason. . . . Ernst Haeckel asserted that science proved both pantheism and monism."[49]

Historically and across cultures, it has been the unique role of religion to offer moral and ethical guidance to humanity. With the preeminence given to science, religion is quickly becoming irrelevant, not only in this regard but even within spiritual matters.

As we have already seen, "the combination of pantheism and its attendant nature worship, religious secrecy, spiritual elitism and hopes of a scientifically assisted evolutionary progress toward a master species has, at some historical junctures, had sinister consequences."[50] Historian R. G. Collingwood

> interprets the rise of fascism and National Socialism in the twentieth century as a direct result of the popularity of neopaganism (i.e., Volkism) in the late 1800s that worshipped the power of the human will and that, in turn, arose to fill a spiritual vacuum created by this very eclipse of faith in orthodox Christianity.[51]

I believe one could safely argue that a similar eclipse is beginning in America.

As the church in Western culture continues to fade from relevance and Christianity becomes increasingly marginalized, there naturally follows a spiritual void, a void that humanity cannot tolerate too long. Thus, encouraged by the progressive principles implicit in modernity (that is, the evolution of spiritual understanding) coupled with the cynicism produced by postmodernity (that is, despair), Westerners are increasingly drawn to fill this spiritual void in terms apart from the biblical God. With the advent of innumerable spiritual options available within New Age, the consumeristic American can peruse the spiritual supermarket for the one that best suits his need. And as "faith" is shifted from the one true God, it will naturally be directed toward self-serving idols and spiritual gurus that promise unlimited power. Unfortunately, as Herrick pointed out, "self-promoting candidates for this position have never been hard to find, nor have their followers been few."[52]

In Genesis, we are told that the temptation that toppled humanity [Adam and Eve] was rooted in the desire to acquire a forbidden knowledge that would make them like God. Sadly, this ancient temptation remains the principal attraction to New Age religious thought. Those who know the one true God do not need to become one. May those of us who have received His marvelous grace and now know Him endeavor to reach and love those still living under the Serpent's deceit.

EPILOGUE

What Are We to Do?

We live in deeply troubled times, and the tendency may be (and, it seems, has been) to withdraw in the face of what appears to be overwhelming forces opposing the gospel. However, retreat is not an option the Lord has given to us. God, in His providence, has placed you and me in this very place, in this very time, and the call of Jesus Christ remains *Follow me!* This is our only option—and should be our only desire if we truly love Him. The last several decades have seen numerous efforts on the part of Christian activists to reverse these deleterious trends, but such efforts have, in the end, accomplished very little. We have seen some victories on the legal and political fronts, and these are no doubt encouraging. A number of polls indicate that advocacy for abortion and same-sex marriage is declining, and I tend to believe that this may be true on some level. However, it remains to be seen whether or not this lack of support will translate into actual public policy measures that once again criminalize abortion and prohibit *any* form of legal recognition for homosexual partnerships. I am inclined to think not. Furthermore, as long as the debate over these issues remains confined to the political arena, there can be no real change in the underlying philosophical consensus that gave rise to them to begin with. As long as our cultural institutions and social structures continue to rest upon a humanistic secular worldview, we will never see sweeping social and cultural change. In addition, the next generation—including many professing Christians—remains largely under the influence of this same secular philosophical consensus. Our past failure to recognize this is, in large part, attributable to the legacy of Christendom. The remedy is for the church in America to both understand the present post-Christendom cultural context and recover an accurate understanding of its mission in light of that reality.

THE LEGACY OF CHRISTENDOM

In granting the Christian church special favors and privileges, the fourth-century Roman emperor Constantine inaugurated the era of the church-state partnership that would profoundly shape European society and culture for centuries to come. As the now protected and privileged religion of society, Christianity would go on to achieve unrivaled social and cultural dominance. The resulting cultures in Europe and later in North America became known as Christendom. Despite the fact that the legal structures of European Christendom were removed in North America (that is, the separation of the state from the church), the legacy of this Constantinian system remained firmly intact by means of common traditions, attitudes, and social structures. (In effect, America was born under a "functional Christendom" that would continue to shape public and private life well into the twentieth century.) Under this Constantinian system, the Christian church would come to occupy a central and influential position in society; the Western world considered itself both formally and officially Christian. So when I speak of post-Christendom, I am making the point that the Christian religion no longer occupies this central place of social and cultural hegemony and the West no longer considers itself to be either formally or officially Christian. This represents a monumental change in the cultural context in which the American church is now attempting to carry out its mission.

What does this new cultural context mean for American Christians, as well as the church and its mission? And given the legacy of Christendom and its eclipse, should we also ask, *What exactly* is *the church's mission?* A proper answer to these two questions is, I think, key to an effective Christian response to the culture that now confronts us. To the first point, the vast majority of American Christians and churches still rest on the assumptions of Christendom, meaning they believe and function as if Christianity still carries the same cultural authority it once did, when this is no longer true. Our brief survey of American culture should convince anyone that Christianity is no longer the nation's central informing influence. As indicated earlier, every cultural institution from education and science, media and the arts, to politics and philosophy is today convincingly secular. Religion in general and Christianity in particular are deliberately excluded from the public square. Christianity has become a marginalized way of thinking that is largely thought to belong to the exclusive realm of one's *private* life. In other words, Christianity is judged irrelevant when it comes to offering any public truth.

CHRISTENDOM AND THE MISSION OF THE CHURCH

I would suggest that the prior reality of Christendom produced what could be called a church-centered, or *ecclesiocentric*,[1] perspective of its mission. Because Christianity was the dominant religion, as well as the consensus view of reality, the emphasis or mission of the church centered more on recruiting members through evangelism, since its social and cultural authority was firmly established. The reality of Christendom would lead the church to view its mission (or *missiology*) as a collateral program of the church; its *de facto* mission would drift toward the institutional maintenance of the church. However, growing and maintaining the church is not the purpose of the Christian, the church, or the gospel. In the wake of recent scholarship, theologians have begun to recover a more comprehensive and orthodox understanding of the church and its mission.

> *We have come to see that mission is not merely an activity of the church. Rather, mission is the result of God's initiative, rooted in God's purposes to restore and heal creation. "Mission" means "sending," and it is the central biblical theme describing the purpose of God in human history. . . . We have begun to learn that the biblical message is more radical, more inclusive, more transforming than we have allowed it to be. . . . We have begun to see that the church of Jesus Christ is not the purpose or goal of the gospel, but rather its instrument and witness. God's mission embraces all of creation.*[2]

In light of this understanding, the point is made that "neither the structures nor the theology of our established Western traditional churches is missional. They are shaped by the legacy of Christendom,"[3] and given the fact that the cultural context is becoming less and less conducive even to member recruitment, the American church is scrambling to define its mission, Christians are increasingly confused as to their purpose, and the gospel message is reduced to a saleslike presentation between "members" and "prospects."

Many churches have recently begun to use the term *missional*, but this is often nothing more than a new word for evangelism operating under the same old assumptions of Christendom. It neither fully considers the post-Christian cultural context or the all-encompassing redemptive mission of God. Because so many churches still labor under the illusion of Christendom, their response to this loss of cultural relevance and missional ineffectiveness ends up being either misguided or reliant upon those very conditions that oppose the gospel, such as modernity. One theologian wrote,

> *The typical North American response to our situation is to analyze the problem and find a solution. These solutions tend to be methodological. Arrange all the components of the church landscape differently, and many assume that the problem can be solved. Or use the best demographic or psychological or sociological insights, and one can redesign the church for success in our changing context.*[4]

This response inevitably results in the church trying to look more like the world in order to be relevant, when what is needed is an intelligent and loving representation of the truth that is relevant to what the world really needs. The latter demands that we better understand the cultural context and dominant ideas (worldviews) that have come to shape our culture, thus, the impetus for this book. As we have seen, these worldviews, which purport to offer an all-embracing life system, must be met with a Christian worldview that offers an "equally comprehensive and far reaching power,"[5] in the words of the late prime minister of the Netherlands, Abraham Kuyper. It is, in large part, the church's present inability to accurately recognize the changing cultural context and assert this all-encompassing view of the Christian faith and message that has rendered Christianity irrelevant. The American church must come to terms with this reality and begin to see itself as existing within a foreign land and, like foreign missionaries, properly *contextualize* its message and mission.

REDISCOVERING THE GOSPEL

Now that we understand that Christendom, with its exclusive social and cultural support of the Christian religion, fostered a narrow church-centered approach to its mission, it is easy to see that it has, in essence, collapsed. And in the wake of Christendom's collapse, what are we as Christians to do? What exactly *is* the church's mission? In order to answer this question, we must first accurately define what we mean by the term *gospel* (or good news). I say "accurately" because I think many Christians—particularly in our highly individualized culture—have come to view the gospel as simply the personal plan of salvation. The modern American emphasis tends toward "fixing the sin problem" in terms that are entirely personal. However, the Scriptures speak in a more comprehensive way that goes far beyond the private version of the gospel that we have come to embrace in the West.

Matthew records the beginning of Jesus' ministry and message with these words: "Jesus began to preach and to say, 'Repent, for *the kingdom of heaven* is at hand'" (4:17). Jesus Himself describes the gospel in relation to the kingdom when He says, "This *gospel of the kingdom* will be preached in all the world" (Matthew 24:14). Matthew described Jesus' ministry by saying, "Jesus went about all Galilee . . . preaching *the gospel of the kingdom*" (4:23). And he reiterated this theme five chapters later: "Then Jesus went about all the cities and villages . . . preaching *the gospel of the kingdom*" (9:35). Jesus told His disciples to "preach, saying, *'The kingdom of heaven* is at hand'" (Matthew 10:7). Mark wrote, "After John [the Baptist] was put in prison, Jesus came . . . preaching *the gospel of the kingdom of God*" (1:14). Philip the apostle "preached the things concerning *the kingdom of God* and the name of Jesus Christ" (Acts 8:12). Paul and Barnabas encouraged new believers to "continue in the faith, . . . saying, 'We must through many tribulations enter *the kingdom of God*'" (Acts 14:22). Paul appeared in the synagogue in Ephesus "reasoning and persuading concerning the things of *the kingdom of God*" (Acts 19:8). Paul, writing about his own ministry, said, "I have gone preaching *the kingdom of God*" (Acts 20:25). While under house arrest, Paul received many visitors to whom he "testified of *the kingdom of God*, persuading them concerning Jesus" (Acts 28:23) (all NKJV, emphasis added).

THE INBREAKING REIGN OF GOD

Clearly, by Jesus' own words and the testimony of the apostles, Jesus was preaching the good news that through Him God's reign, or kingdom, has come and is coming. So the gospel is the fact that in Christ the reign of God is at hand and is *now* breaking into the world. His kingdom, which has come, continues to come forth and will be fully consummated on the day of His return. This is the good news, which offers both a present and future hope to all of God's creation!

Now, this may raise more questions than it answers, most notably, *What exactly is the kingdom (or reign) of God?* A definitive answer to this question is simply not given in Scripture, but we are granted some insights through the teachings of Jesus. First, Jesus made clear that the kingdom has come; when speaking to the Pharisees, He said, "The kingdom of God has come upon you" (Matthew 12:28, NKJV). Again, the commission given to the apostles was to preach that "the kingdom of heaven is at hand" (Matthew 10:7, NKJV). This statement is taken to mean that the kingdom of the Messiah, who is the Lord, is now to be set up according to the Scriptures. To be clear, this "setting up" is entirely the work of God and we are merely His instruments.

Throughout the parables, Jesus used the preface "The kingdom of heaven is like . . ." (see, for example, Matthew 13:31,47). Through parabolic teaching, Jesus described the character and nature of God's ruling reign, which is now only a foretaste of the world to come. The Old Testament's prophetic forecast of the coming day of God envisioned a world characterized by peace, justice, and celebration, in which the full prosperity of the people of God, living under the covenant of God's demanding care and compassionate rule, is realized. The picture given is one of a world full of peace that is grounded in justice. In Jesus' very first sermon recorded by Luke, He entered the synagogue in Nazareth where He had been raised and, taking the book of Isaiah, quoted the following passage:

The Spirit of the Lord is upon me,
  because he has anointed me
  to proclaim good news to the poor.
He has sent me to proclaim liberty to the captives
  and recovering of sight to the blind,
to set at liberty those who are oppressed,
  to proclaim the year of the Lord's favor. (Luke 4:18-19, ESV)

When Jesus finished speaking these words, He closed the book and sat down, and when every eye was "fixed on Him" (verse 20), He said, "Today this Scripture has been fulfilled in your hearing" (verse 21). Can you imagine what it must have been like to hear Jesus speak these words? He was describing the kingdom of God, in which *all* that has resulted from sin and the Fall is being restored by Him! Again, this is the good news! The call upon mankind is to repent and forsake sin so that we might enter the kingdom and be saved. It is the reign of God that the church is sent to bring forth as God's instrument and to which it bears witness in its life and community. The reign of God concerns the whole of creation. This includes society and culture in which the Christian demonstrates the reign of God within a distinct community; serves the world through justice, compassion, and mercy; and proclaims the risen Christ as the only means by which one may enter the kingdom of God.

WHAT IS THE CHURCH'S MISSION?

If the ecclesiocentric view of the church's mission tends to focus on the building of and maintenance of the church (namely, recruiting members by simply sharing the personal plan of salvation), then a proper *theocentric* (or God-centered) view rightly focuses the church and every Christian on the broader mission of God (or *missio Dei*), of which personal salvation is a part. In order for the church to be an effective instrument and faithful witness of the gospel, especially in view of our post-Christian culture, we must recover this God-centered understanding of the church's mission. The mission of the church is not reducible to simply maintaining the institutional church—being missional is not a program of the church, and it is not an activity that occurs only on foreign fields. The church is a body of people who are called together and sent by God into the world to represent His rule and reign: the kingdom of God. The church exists for the mission of God, not for itself!

Dave Lescalleet, my friend and pastor of City Church in Corpus Christi, Texas, described the inbreaking reign of God well when he said,

> *There is a great conversation in Tolkien's epic fantasy* Lord of the Rings *where Samwise is talking to Gandalf and he asks Gandalf a great question: "Will everything sad come untrue?" The kingdom message is Christ (because of His death and resurrection) setting things right again—making everything sad come untrue.*[6]

In essence, the church bears witness to the inbreaking reign of God and serves as the instrument by which God is making everything sad come untrue. There is an optimism that should naturally follow the realization that our God reigns (see Isaiah 52:7). Sadly, this optimism is, in my estimation, largely absent from the evangelical church in America. Many Christians I meet seem to live and think as if Christ has been overcome by the world rather than vice versa (see John 16:33) or that the gates of hell do indeed prevail against His church. Perhaps by recovering the *biblical* mission of the church (as participating in God's unrelenting reign), we can, once again, be a people who live as more than those who seem to be barely surviving!

REPRESENTING GOD'S REIGN

Understanding, then, that the church is *not* the kingdom of God but rather its ambassador, how does the church represent the mission of God in the world? The biblical narrative seems to outline a threefold approach. First, the church demonstrates the reign of God within a distinct community, and second, the church serves the world by doing justice and meeting human needs through compassion and mercy, thereby setting things right. This is where the Christian interpretation of reality becomes essential and why many activist efforts fail. The Christian conceptions of justice provide the intellectual foundations for setting things right in a spirit of love and compassion. Most contemporary attempts at Christian activism rarely consider the intellectual foundations for biblical justice; thus, they fail to provide a substantive or compelling basis for the changes being proposed. In essence, we end up addressing social symptoms rather than the root causes that originate in false conceptions of reality. Further, we rarely do this in a spirit of love and compassion. This, too, likely results from the legacy of Christendom, in which we came to expect certain rights and privileges. Believing these same privileges still exist, we often *demand* respect from the culture as if to earn it would be beneath us. Third and finally, the church is sent to proclaim the message of the risen Christ as the only means by which one may enter the kingdom of God.

DEMONSTRATING GOD'S REIGN

Given that *service* and *proclamation* are fairly self-explanatory, I want to focus on what I believe is both the church's greatest weakness and her greatest challenge today: *demonstrating* the reign of God within a distinct community. Because, as pastor and professor George Hunsberger put it, "before the church is called to do or say anything, it is called and sent to be a unique community of those who live under the reign of God."[7] In a radically individualistic America, this may be the church's greatest obstacle to the *missio Dei*.

Jesus' invitation is to enter the kingdom of God. Practically, this means that we are saved out of our individual isolation and alienation and into the community of faith. Recall that the Great Commission given by Jesus was to "go therefore and make disciples of all nations, baptizing them in the name of the Father and of the Son and of the Holy Spirit" (Matthew 28:19, ESV). Jesus was stressing the conversion of individuals through relationships (that is, make disciples), followed by their being joined to the body of Christ through baptism. There is a "corporateness" to the kingdom message.

Paul stressed that the Gentiles, who were once alienated from "the commonwealth of Israel" (God's covenant people), have been brought near "by the blood of Christ" that "he might create in himself one new man in place of the two, so making peace, and might reconcile us both to God in *one body* through the cross" (Ephesians 2:12-13,15-16, ESV, emphasis added). There is a corporate sense to God's redemptive plan that carries forward from national Israel to form a new covenant of people (the church) — out of both the Jew and Gentile into the new Israel. At the conclusion of Ephesians 2, Paul wrote,

> *You are fellow citizens with the saints and members of the household of God, built on the foundation of the apostles and prophets, Christ Jesus himself being the cornerstone, in whom the* whole structure, being joined together, *grows into a holy temple in the Lord. In him you also are being built* together *into a dwelling place for God by the Spirit. (verses 19-22,* ESV, *emphasis added)*

Again, what's highlighted is the corporate nature of God's redemptive plan and people.

About this, one commentator wrote,

The last verse . . . reminds the readers of the enormous privilege that they are part of this whole construction. They are incorporated in the building, the one universal church, which God makes his dwelling by the Spirit. And they are incorporated in it precisely by union with Christ, in whom all things are being brought into the cosmic harmony and peace enabled by reconciliation inaugurated at the cross.[8]

This community is not merely the social gathering of a people with common values but rather a people who display proof of God's redemptive work in the world. This proof flows forth from converted individuals whose transformation is formed and authenticated through their interaction with other Christians. This community, the church, is intended to bear testimony to the restoration of fellowship with God and each other—a community of self-sacrificing love and support that stands in stark contrast to the fallen world. Jesus Himself established this as the authenticating fact of our faith when he said, "By this all people will know that you are my disciples, if you have love for one another" (John 13:35, ESV). Was this not the preeminent testimony of the first-century church in which they had all things in common?

UNDERMINING AUTHENTICATING COMMUNITY

As Americans, we enter the church with nearly overpowering individualistic inclinations. We come with and cling to expectations and demands that are centered on ourselves. We expect people to talk to and welcome us, but we are unwilling to reach out and talk to them. We have a myriad of petty personal preferences that we impose on the church about worship styles, music, carpet color, and the like. We grade the pastor on whether or not he has met *our* needs through his sermon or kept us attentive. And we certainly aren't interested in anyone getting in our business! We don't humbly submit to one another. We refuse church discipline. We argue, gossip, and divide over inconsequential issues. We attack those outside our traditions, doctrinal convictions, and theological framework; we rarely listen to those with whom we disagree. Often our attitudes and actions toward each other are shameful and bring disgrace on the name of Christ—and we frequently do so in the face of the unbelieving world. We simply do not fulfill this essential part of God's mission because we fail to demonstrate the reign of God within this authenticating community.

If we don't get this right, our service will remain indistinguishable from any other, and our proclamation of the risen Christ will appear shallow and without basis. If we want to overcome our culturalized Christianity to worship and serve the King of kings, we must recover this broader understanding of our mission as Christians in the world. We must learn to properly analyze and intelligently engage the culture, and we must interact with each other and the world in a spirit of grace, love, and charity. The church in America must repent of its radical individualism and independence that separates us from the community of Christ and once again humbly submit to one another. This we *must* do if we want the world to know whose disciples we really are!

CHAPTER 1: The Crisis Confronting the American Church: Rethinking Cultural Engagement

1. David Aikman, *Jesus in Beijing: How Christianity Is Transforming China and the Global Balance of Power* (Washington: Regnery Publishing, 2003), 5.
2. "The Bible/Knowledge," The Barna Group, http://www.barna.org/FlexPage.aspx?Page=Topic&TopicID=7 (accessed February 7, 2006).
3. N. T. Wright, *Evil and the Justice of God* (Downers Grove, IL: InterVarsity, 2006), 119.
4. Norman L. Geisler, *Baker Encyclopedia of Christian Apologetics* (Grand Rapids, MI: Baker, 2002), 154.
5. Geisler, 607.
6. Christopher Lasch, *The Culture of Narcissism: American Life in an Age of Diminishing Expectations* (New York: Norton, 1991), 152.
7. Arthur Allen Leff, "Unspeakable Ethics, Unnatural Law," *Duke Law Journal*, December 1979, 1229–1230.
8. "A Biblical Worldview Has a Radical Effect on a Person's Life," *The Barna Update*, Barna Research Group, December 1, 2003, http://www.barna.org/FlexPage.aspx?Page=BarnaUpdate&BarnaUpdateID=154 (accessed February 7, 2006).

9. "Radical Effect."

10. "Only Half of Protestant Pastors Have a Biblical Worldview," *The Barna Update*, Barna Research Group, January 12, 2004, http://www.barna .org/FlexPage.aspx?Page=BarnaUpdate&BarnaUpdateID=156 (accessed February 7, 2006).

11. "Radical Effect."

12. "American Faith Is Diverse, as Shown Among Five Faith-Based Segments," *The Barna Update*, Barna Research Group, January 29, 2002, http://www.barna.org/FlexPage.aspx?Page= BarnaUpdate&BarnaUpdateID=105 (accessed February 7, 2006).

13. Attributed to the Greek philosopher Protagoras.

14. J. Gresham Machen, "Christianity and Culture," *What Is Christianity? And Other Addresses*, ed. Ned Stonehouse (Grand Rapids, MI: Eerdmans, 1951), 162–163.

15. As quoted in Ed Vitagliano, "The Rebirth of Christianity," *American Family Association Journal* (March 2004): 16.

16. Phillip Jenkins, *The Next Christendom: The Coming of Global Christianity* (New York: Oxford University, 2002), 9.

17. Jenkins, 1, 3.

18. Jenkins, 2.

19. Vitagliano, 16.

20. Vitagliano, 16.

21. Vitagliano, 17.

22. Aikman, 285.

23. Vitagliano, 17.

24. Conducted in 2001 by the Graduate Center of the City University of New York, the "American Religious Identity Survey" reported a decrease in the number of adherents to Christianity from 86.2 percent of the U.S. population in 1990 to 76.5 in 2001. Adherents to Judaism did drop 1.3 percent from 1990 to 2001; however, this is more likely the result of smaller Jewish families and fewer Jewish immigrants. During the same period, of the nineteen religious systems identified and one unclassified, all but Rastafarian experienced growth. The category of "nonreligious" experienced the most growth: up more than double, from approximately 14 million in 1990 to more than 29 million in 2001, indicating the dramatic rise of secularism. Available online at http://www.gc.cuny.edu/ faculty/research_briefs/aris/aris_index.htm (accessed February 7, 2006).

CHAPTER 2: Following Christ in the Modern World: The Challenges of Modernity and Modernism

1. J. Gresham Machen's *The Gospel in the Modern World: And Other Short Writings*, ed. Stephen J. Nichols (Phillipsburg, NJ: P&R Publishing, 2005), 10.

2. Robert B. Reich, "Bush's God," *The American Prospect Online Edition*, July 1, 2004, http://www.prospect.org/cs/articles?articleID=7858 (accessed February 9, 2006).

3. Lesslie Newbigin, *Foolishness to the Greek: The Gospel and Western Culture* (Grand Rapids, MI: Eerdmans, 1986), 63.

4. "Teenagers' Beliefs Moving Farther from Biblical Perspectives," *The Barna Update*, Barna Research Group, October 23, 2000, http://www.barna.org/FlexPage.aspx?Page=BarnaUpdate&BarnaUpdateID=74 (accessed April 25, 2008).

5. "Teenagers' Beliefs."

6. "Americans Are Most Likely to Base Truth on Feelings," *The Barna Update*, Barna Research Group, February 12, 2002, http://www.barna.org/FlexPage.aspx?Page=BarnaUpdate&BarnaUpdateID=106 (accessed April 25, 2008).

7. Josh McDowell, *The Last Christian Generation* (Holiday, FL: Green Key Books, 2006), 34.

8. J. Gresham Machen, *The New Testament: An Introduction to Its Literature and History* (Edinburgh, Scotland: The Banner of Truth Trust, 1976), 377–378.

9. These three impulses were described in an article written January 26, 1993, by John Piper, "Machen's Response to Modernism," http://www.desiringgod.org/ResourceLibrary/Biographies/1464_J_Gresham_Machens_Response_to_Modernism/ (accessed April 16, 2008).

10. Christian Smith, *Soul Searching: The Religious and Spiritual Lives of American Teenagers* (New York: Oxford University, 2005), 162.

11. Smith, 148.

12. Smith, 148.

13. Smith, 162–163. This represents my own summary of the creed of moralistic therapeutic deism as described by the author: (1) A God exists who created and orders the world and watches over human life on earth. (2) God wants people to be good, nice, and fair to each other, as taught in the Bible and by most world religions. (3) The central goal of life is to be happy and feel good about oneself. (4) God does not need to be

particularly involved in one's life except when God is needed to resolve a problem. (5) Good people go to heaven when they die.

14. Smith, 119.

15. Smith, 120.

16. Os Guinness, *No God but God: Breaking with the Idols of Our Age*, ed. John Seel (Chicago: Moody, 1992), 151–174.

17. Post-Enlightenment assumptions in the sense of Enlightenment thinking freed from its Christian influence.

18. G. K. Chesterton, *Heretics* (Nashville: Nelson, 2005), 3.

19. Os Guinness, "Sounding Out the Idols of Church Growth," http://gospel-culture.org.uk/guinness.htm (accessed April 25, 2008).

CHAPTER 3: Postmodernism: An Enemy or Opportunity for the Church?

1. This comparison was made by Keyes during a lecture I attended at L'Abri Fellowship in Southborough, Massachusetts, on January 14, 2004.

2. John Haywood, PhD, *Atlas of World History* (New York: MetroBooks, 2000). Haywood estimates an excess of 50 million deaths directly related to World War II and another 15 million to World War I.

3. Iosif G. Dyadkin, *Unnatural Deaths in the USSR, 1928–1954* (New Brunswick: Transaction Books, 1983). Fifty-six to 62 million "unnatural deaths" are estimated for the USSR overall, with 34 to 49 million under Stalin.

4. Robert L. Walker, "The Human Cost of Communism in China," A Study of the Committee on the Judiciary United States Senate (Washington, DC: Government Printing Office, 1971). Some estimates are as high as 72 million; however, Walker estimated between 34.3 and 68.73 million.

5. Richard Pipes, *A Concise History of the Russian Revolution* (New York: Vintage Books, 1995). Pipes estimates 9 million deaths between 1917 and 1922.

6. John Shattuck, assistant U.S. secretary of state for human rights, in a speech delivered at the Stanford Forum, sponsored by the Stanford Committee on Law and Human Rights, May 2, 1995, http://www.stanford.edu/dept/news/pr/95/950502Arc5252.html (accessed February 14, 2006).

7. Stéphane Courtois and others, *The Black Book of Communism: Crimes, Terror, Repression*, trans. Jonathan Murphy and Mark Kramer (Boston:

Harvard University, 1999). This figure of approximately 100 million is drawn from the authors' estimated death tolls as follows: 65 million in China; 20 million in the Soviet Union; 2 million in North Korea; 2 million in Cambodia; 1.7 million in Africa, 1.5 million in Afghanistan, 1 million in Vietnam, 1 million in the Communist states of Eastern Europe, and 150,000 in Latin America.

8. Molly Billings, "The Influenza Pandemic of 1918," Human Virology Department, Stanford University, June 1997, http://www.stanford.edu/group/virus/uda/ (accessed February 22, 2006).

9. Jennifer Brower and Peter Chalk, "The Spread of Global Pathogens Can Imperil Us All," Rand Corporation Report, August 18, 2005, http://www.rand.org/publications/randreview/issues/summer2003/vectors.html (accessed February 14, 2006).

10. "Understanding Poverty," The World Bank, http://web.worldbank.org/WBSITE/EXTERNAL/TOPICS/EXTPOVERTY/0,,contentMDK:20153855~menuPK:373757~pagePK:148956~piPK:216618~theSitePK:336992,00.html (accessed February 14, 2006).

11. J. P. Moreland and William Lane Craig, *Philosophical Foundations for a Christian Worldview* (Downers Grove, IL: InterVarsity, 2003), 145.

12. Moreland and Craig, 145.

13. Moreland and Craig, 132.

14. Rousseau argued that the state of nature was the present state of all the other animals and the condition man was in before the creation of civilization and society and that good people are made unhappy and corrupted by their experiences in society.

15. Moreland and Craig, 145.

16. "Hardwired to Connect: The New Scientific Case for Authoritative Communities," a report from the Commission on Children at Risk, Dartmouth Medical School, 2003.

17. "Hardwired to Connect," 8, quoting from "Child Health 2000: New Pediatrics in the Changing Environment of Children's Needs in the 21st Century," Pediatrics 96 (1995): 807.

18. "Hardwired," 8.

19. "Hardwired," 9.

20. "Hardwired," 5.

21. "Hardwired," 5.

22. "Hardwired," 5.

23. "Hardwired," 7.

Chapter 4: Consumerism: Idolatry Is Alive and Well!

1. Timothy V. Vaverek, "Christian Asceticism: Breaking Consumerism's Destructive Hold," *Houston Catholic Worker* 21, no. 1 (January 2001), http://www.cjd.org/paper/consum.html.

2. Richard John Neuhaus, *Doing Well and Doing Good: The Challenge to the Christian Capitalist* (New York: Doubleday, 1992), 52–53.

3. Christopher Lasch, *The Culture of Narcissism: American Life in an Age of Diminishing Expectations* (New York: Norton, 1979), 152.

4. Raymond J. de Souza, "John Paul II and the Problem of Consumerism," Acton Institute, http://www.acton.org/publicat/randl/article.php?id=321 (accessed February 17, 2006).

5. "Snapshot for July 7, 2004," Economic Snapshots, Economic Policy Institute, http://www.epinet.org/content.cfm/webfeatures _snapshots_07072004 (accessed February 20, 2006).

6. "Table 2. Time spent in primary activities . . . 2006 annual averages," Department of Labor, Bureau of Labor Statistics news release, http://www.bls.gov/news.release/atus.t02.htm (accessed February 20, 2006).

7. L. C. Sayer, S. M. Bianchi, and J. P. Robinson, "Are Parents Investing Less in Children? Trends in Mothers' and Fathers' Time with Children," a paper presented at the American Sociological Association annual meeting, August 2000, Washington, DC, quoting the Council of Economic Advisors Report, 1999, http://www.ccpr.ucla.edu/docs/Bianchi %20article.pdf (accessed February 20, 2006). Note: The estimate of a twenty-two-hour decline between 1969 and 1999 in parental time in caring for children was arrived at by subtracting increased employment hours of parents from total waking hours. This approach has been questioned by some sociologists, but for the purposes of demonstrating that increased time at work obviously results in reduced time with family, I believe it makes the point.

8. W. Bradford Cox, "Analysis: Religion, Family, and the General Social Survey," October 19, 2005, episode no. 908, http://www.pbs.org/wnet/ religionandethics/week908/analysis1.html (accessed February 22, 2006).

9. Francis A. Schaeffer, *How Should We Then Live?* video series (Muskegon, MI: Gospel Communications, August 16, 2007).

10. Blaise Pascal, *Pascal's Pensées* (New York: Pantheon Books, 1965), 107.

11. Pascal, 57.

12. Quoted in Carlin Flora, "Consumerism: One Choice Too Many," *Psychology Today* (January/February 2004), http://psychologytoday.com/

rss/pto-20040116-000001.html.

13. David G. Myers, "The funds, friends, and faith of happy people," *American Psychologist* 55, no. 1 (January 2000): 56.

14. Vaverek.

15. Vaverek.

16. Vaverek.

17. Michael Medved, taken from a lecture delivered on March 9, 2005, on the Hillsdale College campus and printed in the May 2005 *Imprimis* newsletter.

18. "Evangelicals Are the Most Generous Givers, but Fewer Than 10% of Born Again Christians Give 10% to Their Church," *The Barna Update*, Barna Research Group, April 5, 2000, http://www.barna.org/FlexPage .aspx?Page=BarnaUpdate&BarnaUpdateID=52 (accessed February 22, 2006). Barna reports that the median amount of money given to nonprofits and churches by the typical adult last year was $300. That is a 14 percent decline from 1998 levels ($350 median per person). Even more telling was the decline in the mean total gift amount: average for 1999 was $1,045 per adult. That represents a 24 percent decline from 1998, when the average cumulative giving was $1,377.

19. "Evangelicals Generous Givers."

20. "Evangelicals Generous Givers."

21. Vaverek.

22. G. K. Chesterton, *What's Wrong with the World* (San Francisco: Ignatius Press, 1994), 37.

CHAPTER 5: The Sexualized Culture and Its Contribution to Unbelief

1. Martin Luther, *Luther's Works. Weimar Edition. Briefwechsel* [Correspondence], vol. 3, 81–82.

2. J. P. Moreland and William Lane Craig, *Philosophical Foundations for a Christian Worldview* (Downers Grove, IL: InterVarsity, 2003), 132.

3. Moreland and Craig, 132.

4. Moreland and Craig, 132.

5. Francis A. Schaeffer, *Francis A. Schaeffer Trilogy: The Three Essential Books in One Volume* (Wheaton, IL: Crossway, 1990), 155.

6. Pitirim A. Sorokin, *The American Sex Revolution* (Boston: Porter Sargent, 1956), 65. Sorokin affirms that the Freudian theory "teaches that repression of incestuous or otherwise illicit sex impulses is the main source of psychoneurosis."

7. J. D. Unwin, *Sex and Culture* (London: Oxford University, 1934), 411–412, 431–432.

8. Unwin, *Sex and Culture*, 324–326.

9. J. D. Unwin, "Sexual Regulations and Cultural Behavior," address given on March 27, 1935, to the medical section of the British Psychological Society, later printed by Oxford University Press. Unwin stated, "In human records there is no case of an absolutely monogamous society failing to display great energy." Unwin further observed that "expansive energy has never been displayed by a generation that inherited a modified monogamy, modified polygamy, or an absolute polygamy."

10. Unwin, "Sexual Regulations."

11. Unwin, "Sexual Regulations."

12. Margaret Sanger, *The Pivot of Civilization* (New York: Brentano's, 1922), 270–271.

13. Margaret Sanger, "A Plan for Peace," *Birth Control Review* (April 1932): 106.

14. Margaret Sanger, "The Eugenic Value of Birth Control Propaganda," *Birth Control Review* (October 1921): 5.

15. Alfred Charles Kinsey, Wardell B. Pomeroy, and Clyde E. Martin, *Sexual Behavior in the Human Male* (Philadelphia: W. B. Saunders, 1948), 18.

16. W. G. Cochran, F. Mosteller, J. W. Tukey, and W. O. Jenkins, "Statistical Problems of the Kinsey Report: A Report of the American Statistical Association Committee to Advise the National Research Council Committee for Research in Problems of Sex" (Washington: The American Statistical Association, 1954), 18.

17. Quoted in Arno Karlen, *Sexuality and Homosexuality: A New View* (New York: W. W. Horton, 1971), 456.

18. Quoted in Judith A. Reisman, *Kinsey: Crimes and Consequences* (Institute for Media Education, 1998, 2000), 64. Reisman received a copy of this private letter, dated December 6, 1990, during her deposition.

19. Quoted in Reisman, ii.

20. Reisman, 222.

21. Abraham Stone and Norman E. Himes, *Planned Parenthood: A Practical Handbook of Birth-Control Methods* (New York: Collier, 1965), 235.

22. Reisman, 248.

23. Kinsey, Pomeroy, and Martin, 678.

24. Hugh Hefner, editorial, *Playboy*, January 1989.

25. Judith A. Reisman, *Soft Porn Plays Hardball: Its Tragic Effects on Women, Children, and the Family* (Lafayette, LA: Huntington House, 1991), 78.

26. Leonore Weitzman, *The Divorce Revolution: The Unexpected Social and Economic Consequences for Women and Children in America* (New York: Free Press, 1985), overleaf.

27. S. Singh and J. E. Darroch, "Adolescent pregnancy and childbearing levels and trends in developed countries," *Family Planning Perspectives* 32, no. 1 (January/February 1999): 14–23, http://www.guttmacher.org/pubs/journals/3201400.html (accessed April 28, 2008).

28. American Social Health Association and the Kaiser Family Foundation, *Sexually Transmitted Diseases in America: How Many Cases and at What Cost?* (Menlo Park: Kaiser Family Foundation, 1998), http://www.kff.org/womenshealth/1445-std_qa.cfm (accessed April 28, 2008).

29. Mary Calderone and Eric Johnson, *The Family Book About Sexuality* (New York: Harper & Row, 1981), 171.

30. Eric Schlosser, "The Business of Pornography," *U.S. News and World Report* (February 10, 1997): 44.

31. American Social Health Association. Complete report available free from the Henry J. Kaiser Family Foundation (800-656-4533), publication 1445.

32. T. R. Eng and W. T. Butler, eds., Institute of Medicine, *The Hidden Epidemic: Confronting the Sexually Transmitted Disease* (Washington: National Academy Press, 1997).

33. F. X. Bosch and others, "Prevalence of human papillomavirus in cervical cancer: a worldwide perspective," for the International Biological Study on Cervical Cancer (IBSCC) Study Group, *Journal of the National Cancer Institute* 87 (1995): 796–802.

34. "Cancer Facts and Figures 2000: Selected Cancers," American Cancer Society, http://www.cancer.org/statistics/cff2000/selected cancers.html (accessed April 30, 2008).

35. "Teen Birth Rates: How Does the United Sates Compare?" National Campaign to Prevent Teen Pregnancy, TeenPregnancy.org, http://www.teenpregnancy.org/resources/reading/pdf/inatl_comparisons2006.pdf (accessed April 30, 2008). Despite a one-third decline since the early 1990s, the United States still has the highest rates of teen pregnancy and birth among comparable countries as of 2004.

36. "FBI Crime Report, 1993," FBI Uniform Crime Report, National Crime

Survey, U.S. Department of Justice, 1990.

37. *Final Report of the Attorney General's Commission on Pornography* (Nashville: Rutledge Hill Press, 1986), 261.

38. William O'Donohue and James H. Geer, eds., *The Sexual Abuse of Children: Clinical Issues, Volume 2* (Hillsdale, NJ: Lawrence Erlbaum Associates, 1992), 5.

39. "Predators: What's Really Behind Today's Teacher-Student Epidemic of Sex," WorldNetDaily.com (March 1, 2006), http://www.worldnetdaily .com/news/article.asp?ARTICLE_ID=49049 (accessed March 2, 2006).

40. "Abortion in the United States: Statistics and Trends," National Right to Life, http://www.nrlc.org/ABORTION/facts/abortionstats.html (accessed April 30, 2008).

41. Unwin, "Sexual Regulations."

42. Unwin, "Sexual Regulations."

43. "Homosexual Relations," Gallup Poll, May 2005, http://poll.gallup .com/content/default.aspx?ci=1651&pg=1 (accessed April 25, 2006).

44. Barbara Dafoe Whitehead and David Popenoe, "The State of Our Unions: The Social Health of Marriage in America, 2005" National Marriage Project, Rutgers University, 2005, http://marriage.rutgers.edu/ Publications/SOOU/TEXTSOOU2005.htm#Fragile_Families (accessed April 25, 2006).

45. Janice Shaw Crouse, "Leaving on a Jet Plane: Illegitimacy Trends and the Nation's Children," Beverly LaHaye Institute, January 16, 2004, http://www.cwfa.org/articledisplay.asp?id=5109&department =BLI&categoryid=femfacts (accessed April 25, 2006).

46. Whitehead and Popenoe, 2005.

47. Whitehead and Popenoe, 2005.

CHAPTER 6: Homosexuality: Thinking Critically and Acting Compassionately

1. "Born Again Adults Remain Firm in Opposition to Abortion and Gay Marriage," *The Barna Update*, Barna Research, July 23, 2001, http:// www.barna.org/FlexPage.aspx?Page=BarnaUpdate&BarnaUpdateID=94 (accessed April 30, 2008).

2. William M. Byne, MD, PhD, "Born Gay," ProCon.org, http://www .borngayprocon.org/BiosInd/williambyne.html (accessed March 7, 2008).

3. "Is There a 'Gay Gene'?" National Association for Research and Therapy of Homosexuality (NARTH), http://www.narth.com/docs/istheregene

.html (accessed March 7, 2008). This article was adapted from two sources: a paper titled "The Gay Gene?" by Jeffrey Satinover, MD, in *The Journal of Human Sexuality*, 1996 (available by calling 972-713-7130); and past issues of the NARTH Bulletin. For an in-depth discussion of homosexuality and genetics, consult Dr. Satinover's 1996 book *Homosexuality and the Politics of Truth* (Hamewith/Baker).

4. C. Mann, "Genes and Behavior," *Science* 264 (1994): 1687.

5. J. Michael Bailey and Richard C. Pillard, "A Genetic Study of Male Sexual Orientation," *Archives of General Psychiatry* 48 (December 1991): 1089, 1094.

6. P. Billings and J. Beckwith, *Technology Review* (July 1993): 60.

7. Scott L. Hershberger, "A Twin Registry Study of Male and Female Sexual Orientation," *The Journal of Sex Research* 34, no. 2 (1997): 212.

8. Simon LeVay, "A Difference in Hypothalamic Structure Between Heterosexual and Homosexual Men," *Science* 253, no. 1054 (August 30, 1991): 1034–1037.

9. Joe Dallas, "Responding to Pro-Gay Theology," LeadershipU.com, http://www.leaderu.com/jhs/dallas.html (accessed April 21, 2008).

10. Quoted in Dallas.

11. LeVay, 1037.

12. Dallas.

13. Quoted in A. Dean Byrd, Shirley E. Cox, Jeffrey W. Robinson, "The Innate-Immutable Argument Finds No Basis in Science" (updated February 8, 2008), National Association for Research and Therapy of Homosexuality (NARTH), http://www.narth.com/docs/innate.html (accessed March 7, 2008).

14. John Horgan, "Gay Genes Revisited: Doubts Arise over Research on the Biology of Homosexuality," *Scientific American* (November 1995): 26.

15. Anastasia Toufexis, "New Evidence of a 'Gay Gene'" *Time* 146, no. 20 (November 13, 1995): 95.

16. "Is There a 'Gay Gene'?"

17. Miron Baron, "Genetic Linkage and Male Homosexual Orientation," *British Medical Journal* 307 (August 7, 1993): 337.

18. Dallas.

19. Dallas.

20. Dallas.

21. Byrd, Cox, and Robinson.

22. William Byne and Bruce Parsons, "Human Sexual Orientation: The

Biologic Theories Reappraised," *Archives of General Psychiatry* 50 (March 1993): 236.

23. Byne and Parsons, 236.
24. Daniel G. Brown, "Homosexuality and Family Dynamics," *Bulletin of the Menninger Clinic* 27, no. 5 (September 1963): 232.
25. James R. Bramblett Jr. and Carol Anderson Darling, "Sexual Contacts: Experiences, Thoughts, and Fantasies of Adult Male Survivors of Child Sexual Abuse," *Journal of Sex and Marital Therapy* 23, no. 4 (Winter 1997): 313.
26. Karla Jay and Allen Young, *The Gay Report: Lesbians and Gay Men Speak Out About Sexual Experiences and Lifestyles* (New York: Summit Books, 1979), 249.
27. Jay and Young, 248.
28. Jay and Young, 248.
29. Jay and Young, 340.
30. Jay and Young, 302.
31. Jay and Young, 587.
32. Jay and Young, 555.
33. Jay and Young, 260.
34. Mel Seesholtz, "Part II: The Evangelical Christian Right's Pathological Attack on America," Counterbias.com, January 4, 2006, http://www.counterbias.com/505.html (accessed April 30, 2008).
35. "Increases in Unsafe Sex and Rectal Gonorrhea Among Men Who Have Sex with Men—San Francisco, CA, 1994–1997," *Mortality and Morbidity Weekly Report*, Centers for Disease Control and Prevention (January 29, 1999): 45.
36. A. P. Bell, M. S. Weinberg, and S. K. Hammersmith, *Sexual Preference* (Bloomington: Indiana University Press, 1981), 308.
37. David McWhirter and Andrew Mattison, *The Male Couple: How Relationships Develop* (Englewood Cliffs, NJ: Prentice-Hall, 1984), 252–253.
38. "Increases in Unsafe Sex," 45.
39. Edward O. Laumann and others, *The Sexual Organization of the City* (Chicago: The University of Chicago, 2004), 108.
40. Laumann and others, 109.
41. "Table 9. Male Adult/Adolescent AIDS Cases by Exposure Category and Race/Ethnicity, Reported Through December 2001, United States," Centers for Disease Control and Prevention, Division of HIV/AIDS

Prevention, http://www.cdc.gov/hiv/stats/hasr1302.pdf.

42. B. A. Koblin, J. M. Morrison, P. E. Taylor, R. L. Stoneburner, and C. E. Stevens, "Mortality Trends in a Cohort of Homosexual Men in New York City, 1978–1988," *American Journal of Epidemiology* 136, no. 6 (1992): 646–656.

43. Robert S. Hogg and others, "Modeling the Impact of HIV Disease on Mortality in Gay and Bisexual Men," *International Journal of Epidemiology* 26 (1997): 657.

44. D. J. McKirnan and P. Peterson, "Alcohol and Drug Use Among Homosexual Men and Women: Epidemiology and Population Characteristics," *Addictive Behavior* 14 (1989): 545–553.

45. J. Bradford, C. Ryan, and E. D. Rothblum, "National Lesbian Health Care Survey: Implications for Mental Health Care," *Journal of Consulting and Clinical Psychology* 62, no. 2 (1994): 228–242.

46. Peter Kreeft, *How to Win the Culture War: A Christian Battle Plan for a Society in Crisis* (Downers Grove, IL: InterVarsity, 2002), 51.

47. Peter Kreeft, "Your Inner Cop," *Crisis Magazine* 19, no. 5 (May 2001), http://www.catholiceducation.org/articles/civilization/cc0098.html.

48. Kreeft, *Culture War*, 51.

49. Kreeft, *Culture War*, 49.

50. Quoted in William B. Rubenstein, *Since When Is Marriage a Path to Liberation? Lesbians, Gay Men, and the Law* (New York: New York Press, 1993), 398, 400.

CHAPTER 7: Why Is Marriage Important? The Reasonable Defense of Marriage

1. Barbara Dafoe Whitehead and David Popenoe, "The State of Our Unions, The Social Health of Marriage in America, 2002," The National Marriage Project (Rutgers, the State University of New Jersey, http://marriage.rutgers.edu/Publications/SOOU/TEXTSOOU2002.htm (accessed May 1, 2008).

2. Robert P. George, *The Clash of Orthodoxies: Law, Religion, and Morality in Crisis* (Wilmington, DE: ISI Books, 2001), 77.

3. Quoted in Robert P. George, 77–78.

4. A. Milan, "One hundred years of families," *Statistics Canada* (2000), *Canadian Social Trends,* No. 11–008, 56.

5. As quoted by Robert Browning in a book review of *The Case for Marriage: Why Married People Are Happier, Healthier, and Better Off Financially,* by Linda Waite and Maggie Gallagher, http://www

.religion-online.org/showarticle.asp?title=2101 (accessed May 1, 2008).

6. Linda Waite and Maggie Gallagher, *The Case for Marriage: Why Married People Are Happier, Healthier, and Better Off Financially* (New York: Broadway Books, 2000), 47.

7. Waite and Gallagher, 50.

8. Waite and Gallagher, 79.

9. Waite and Gallagher, 79.

10. Waite and Gallagher, 155.

11. Kersti Yllo and Murray A. Strauss, "Interpersonal Violence Among Married and Cohabitating Couples," *Family Relations* 30 (1981): 343.

12. Waite and Gallagher, 152.

13. William G. Axinn and Arlan Thorton, "The Relationship Between Cohabitation and Divorce: Selectivity or Casual Influence?" *Demography* 29 (1992): 357–374.

14. Elizabeth Thomson and Ugo Colella, "Cohabitation and Marital Stability: Quality or Commitment?" *Journal of Marriage and the Family* 54 (1992): 259–267.

15. Thomson and Colella, 263.

16. Alan Booth and David Johnson, "Premarital Cohabitation and Marital Success," *Journal of Family Issues* 9 (1988): 261.

17. Neil G. Bennett, Ann Klimas Blanc, and David Bloom, "Commitment and the Modern Union: Assessing the Link Between Premarital Cohabitation and Subsequent Marital Stability," *American Sociological Review* 53 (1988): 127–138.

18. Margaret A. Segrest and M. O'Neal Weeks, "Comparison of the Role Expectations of Married and Cohabitating Subjects," *International Journal of Sociology and the Family* 6 (1976): 275–281.

19. John D. Cunningham and John K. Antill, "Cohabitation and Marriage: Retrospective and Predictive Comparisons," *Journal of Social and Personal Relationships* 11 (1994): 89.

20. Waite and Gallagher, 110–123.

21. Waite and Gallagher, 135.

22. Stanley Kurtz, "The End of Marriage in Scandinavia: The 'conservative case' for same-sex marriage collapses," *The Weekly Standard* (February 2, 2004), http://www.weeklystandard.com/Content/Public/Articles/000/000/003/660zypwj.asp.

23. Kurtz.

24. Kurtz.

25. Kurtz.

26. Kurtz.

27. Kurtz.

28. Kurtz.

29. Kurtz.

30. Mary Ann Glendon, "For Better or for Worse? The federal marriage amendment would strike a blow for freedom," opinion post to online editorial page, *The Wall Street Journal* (February 25, 2004), http://www .opinionjournal.com/editorial/feature.html?id=110004735 (accessed May 1, 2008).

CHAPTER 8: Feminism: Refuting Christianity as Oppressive to Women

1. Murtaza Mandli-Yadav, "Mixed findings on progress for women," Third World Network, no. 97, September 1998, http://www.twnside.org.sg/ title/mixed-cn.htm (accessed February 2, 2007).

2. "Women's Rights in the Middle East and North Africa," Women's Rights, Human Rights Watch, http://www.hrw.org/women/overview -mena.html (accessed February 2, 2007).

3. Alvin J. Schmidt, *How Christianity Changed the World* (Grand Rapids, MI: Zondervan, 2001), 121.

4. "Women and Violence," United Nations Department of Public Information DPI/1772/HR, February 1996, http://www.un.org/rights/ dpi1772e.htm (accessed May 2, 2008).

5. "Women's Rights in Asia," Women's Rights, Human Rights Watch, http://www.hrw.org/women/overview-asia.html (accessed February 2, 2007).

6. "Women's Rights in the Middle East and North Africa."

7. *New Catholic Encyclopedia* (New York: McGraw-Hill, 1967), s.v. "woman" (by L. F. Cervantes).

8. Mardi Keyes, *Feminism and the Bible* (Downers Grove, IL: InterVarsity Press, 1995), 3.

9. Leonard Swidler, "Jesus Was a Feminist," quoted in reprint by Christians for Biblical Equality (380 Lafayette Rd. South, Suite 122, St. Paul, MN 55107), 1.

10. Keyes, *Feminism*, 4.

11. This quote was adapted from a lecture that I attended at L'Abri Fellowship in Southborough, Massachusetts, on January 16, 2004, by Mardi Keyes, titled "Feminism and the Bible."

12. Keyes, *Feminism*, 5–6.
13. Keyes, *Feminism*, 7.
14. Keyes, *Feminism*, 7.
15. Keyes, *Feminism*, 7–8.
16. Keyes, *Feminism*, 9.
17. Dorothy L. Sayers, *Are Women Human?* (Grand Rapids, MI: Eerdmans, 1971), 47.
18. Sayers, 11.
19. Keyes lecture.
20. Susan Brownmiller, *Against Our Will: Men, Women, and Rape* (New York: Simon & Schuster, 1975), 14–15. "The male ideology of rape is a conscious process of intimidation by which all men keep all women in a state of fear."
21. Quoted from a review of Marilyn French's book *The War Against Women* (New York: Summit Books, 1992). The reviewer is Karen Lehrman in "Tactical Errors," from *The Women's Review of Books* X, no. 2 (November 1992).
22. Andrea Dworkin, *Intercourse* (New York: Basic Books, 1987), 122–124.
23. Keyes lecture.
24. Keyes, *Feminism*, 18.
25. Keyes lecture.
26. Keyes lecture.
27. Quoted in Keyes, *Feminism,* 21.
28. Keyes, *Feminism*, 22.

CHAPTER 9: New Age Spirituality: Filling the Spiritual Vacuum

1. *Webster's Ninth New Collegiate Dictionary*, s.v. "monism."
2. Art Lindsley, *True Truth: Defending Absolutes in a Relativistic World* (Downers Grove, IL: InterVarsity, 2004), 107.
3. Lindsley, 107.
4. Lindsley, 107.
5. Quoted in James A. Herrick, *The Making of the New Spirituality: The Eclipse of the Western Religious Tradition* (Downers Grove, IL: InterVarsity, 2003), 162.
6. Herrick, 15.
7. Herrick, 15.
8. "The American Religious Identity Survey," graduate center, City University of New York, 2001, http://www.gc.cuny.edu/faculty/

research_briefs/aris/aris_index.htm (accessed March 5, 2007).

9. Herrick, 17.

10. Herrick, 17.

11. Eckhart Tolle, *A New Earth: Awakening to Your Life's Purpose* (New York: Penguin Group, 2006), 315.

12. "Biography," Eckhart Tolle website, http://eckharttolle.com/eckhart _biography (accessed May 2, 2008).

13. "Biography."

14. Marianne Williamson, *A Course in Miracles*, http://www2.oprah.com/ xm/mwilliamson/mwilliamson_archive.jhtml (accessed May 2, 2008).

15. *The Teaching of the Buddha* (Tokyo: Bukkyo Dendo Kyokai, 1968), 86, 100, 104, 108.

16. All quotations here from *A Course in Miracles*, http://www2.oprah.com/ xm/mwilliamson/mwilliamson_archive.jhtml (accessed May 2, 2008).

17. Herrick, 14.

18. Quoted in Herrick, 14.

19. Herrick, 14.

20. Herrick, 18.

21. See John Edward, http://www.johnedward.net (accessed February 2007).

22. Dan Brown, *The Da Vinci Code: A Novel* (New York: Doubleday, 2003), front matter.

23. This quote was taken from a talk given by Dan Brown at the New Hampshire Writers Project. A link to this audio is available at http:// www.danbrown.com/novels/davinci_code/faqs.html (accessed March 6, 2007).

24. "Feng Shui: The Art of Placement," Wind and Water, Inc., http://www .artoffengshuiinc.com (accessed March 5, 2007).

25. "Coming Soon: The Feng Shui Phone, courtesy of Motorola," Wireless-Watch.Community, http://wireless-watch.com/2006/04/29/coming -soon-the-feng-shui-phone-courtesy-of-motorola/ (accessed March 5, 2007).

26. Quoted in Herrick, 19.

27. Herrick, 19.

28. As quoted by Chuck Colson, "An Old Error in a New Package," Breakpoint Commentaries, May 14, 2004, http://www.breakpoint.org/ listingarticle.asp?ID=5095 (accessed May 2, 2008).

29. "The American Religious Identity Survey."

30. John Ankerberg and John Weldon, *Encyclopedia of Cults and New Religions: Jehovah's Witnesses, Mormonism, Mind Sciences, Baha'i, Zen, Unitarianism* (Eugene, OR: Harvest House, 1999), 59.

31. Herrick, 191.

32. Herrick, 192.

33. Herrick, 192.

34. Herrick, 194.

35. Herrick, 194.

36. Herrick, 194.

37. Herrick, 193.

38. Herrick, 193.

39. George L. Mosse, *The Crisis of German Ideology: Intellectual Origins of the Third Reich* (New York: Grosset and Dunlap, 1964), 6.

40. Herrick, 33.

41. Dan Brown, "The Da Vinci Code: What's Happening with the Da Vinci Code?" http://www.danbrown.com/novels/davinci_code/pub_weekly .html (accessed May 2, 2008).

42. Herrick, 34.

43. Herrick, 34.

44. Herrick, 34.

45. Herrick, 34.

46. Herrick, 34.

47. Herrick, 34.

48. John Stott, *The Contemporary Christian: An Urgent Plea for Double Listening* (Downers Grove, IL: InterVarsity, 1992), 15.

49. Stott, 262.

50. Stott, 280.

51. Richard Noll, *The Jung Cult: Origins of a Charismatic Movement* (Princeton, NJ: Princeton University Press, 1994), 38.

52. Herrick, 280.

EPILOGUE: What Are We to Do?

1. Darrell L. Guder, ed., *Missional Church: A Vision for the Sending of the Church in North America* (Grand Rapids, MI: Eerdmans, 1998), 4.

2. Guder, 4–5.

3. Guder, 5.

4. Guder, 2.

5. Abraham Kuyper, *Lectures on Calvinism* (Grand Rapids, MI: Eerdmans, 1931), 11.
6. This story is taken from a conversation with the author on March 13, 2008.
7. Guder, 103.
8. D. A. Carson, R. T. France, J. A. Motyer, and G. J. Wenham, eds., "Ephesians 2:11–22: A digression: the church, cosmic reconciliation and unity: the new temple," *New Bible Commentary* (Downers Grove, IL: InterVarsity, 1953).

AUTHOR

S. MICHAEL CRAVEN is the president of the Center for Christ and Culture located in Dallas, Texas, where he studies, writes, and lectures on the relevant intersection of theology, philosophy, and culture. A leading cultural apologist, he offers a rational biblical response to the various cultural forces that seek to reshape the philosophical consensus in America.

Craven has authored numerous publications and articles; has been a featured speaker at national conferences, universities, and seminaries; and appeared on Fox News, CNN, ABC, NBC, and other national television and radio programs. His popular commentaries are syndicated on *Crosswalk.com*, *Christianity.com*, and *ChristianPost.com*.

Craven is an occasional guest host of the nationally syndicated radio program *Point of View* and serves as an adjunct professor at Western Seminary in San Jose, California, teaching a course of his own design, "How to Maximize the Church's Redemptive Influence." He also is a senior fellow of cultural and family issues at the Center for Cultural Leadership in Santa Cruz, California, and served as the moderator of the Fellowship of Mere Christianity.

Study more about cultural change with other titles by NavPress!

Refractions
Makoto Fujimura
978-1-60006-301-5

Move away from the "culture wars" language. In a series of essays, Makoto Fujimura helps to understand the connection between faith, art, and culture. Find inspiration and experience a call to engage faith with culture through art.

Coffeehouse Theology
Ed Cyzewski
978-1-60006-277-3

In today's culture, there is a barrier of ignorance and misunderstanding in the study of God. Ed Cyzewski seeks to build a method for theology that is rooted in a relationship with God and thrives on dialogue. Through stories and illustrations, you'll gather the basic tools needed to study God. Study guide and discussion guide also available.

The God Who Smokes
Timothy J. Stoner
978-1-60006-247-6

Emergent theology is raising some of the most provocative and divisive questions in the church today. *The God Who Smokes* imagines a twenty-first-century church where hope hangs with holiness, passion sits next to purity, and compassion can relate to character. Join Timothy J. Stoner as he provides an honest response to the postmodern cry for authentic spirituality.

To order copies, call NavPress at 1-800-366-7788
or log on to www.navpress.com.